Phony Communism Is Dead...
Long Live Real Communism

Other books by Bob Avakian

*The Loss in China and the Revolutionary Legacy
of Mao Tsetung*

Mao Tsetung's Immortal Contributions

*For a Harvest of Dragons: On the "Crisis of Marxism"
and the Power of Marxism, Now More Than Ever*

A Horrible End, or an End to the Horror?

*Bullets from the Writings, Speeches, and Interviews
of Bob Avakian, Chairman of the
Revolutionary Communist Party, USA*

Democracy: Can't We Do Better Than That?

Reflections, Sketches & Provocations

*In the Aftermath of the Persian Gulf War, More on
Could We Really Win?*

Phony Communism Is Dead... Long Live Real Communism

by Bob Avakian

RCP Publications • Chicago

RCP Publications
P.O. Box 3486, Chicago, IL 60654

©1992 by RCP Publications. All rights reserved
Printed in USA

ISBN 0-89851-112-7

Table of Contents

Publisher's Preface   i

Introduction   1

Chapter 1
The "Demise of Communism"—and the Communist Future   9

The Three Milestones   11

   MARX   11

     Historical Materialism—The Pivotal Point of Marxism   12

     The Dirty Little Secret of Capitalist Exploitation   19

   LENIN   23

     Political Economy of Imperialism   24

     The Vanguard Party of the Proletariat   27

     The Further Development of Proletarian Revolution
     as a World Revolutionary Process   29

   MAO   33

     The Theory and Strategy of
     New-Democratic Revolution   33

     Continuing the Revolution
     Under the Dictatorship of the Proletariat   35

   MARXISM-LENINISM-MAOISM: A Synthesis,
   Omnipotent Because It Is True   39

The Current Assault Against Marxism:
Distortions and Refutations   40

     The Myth of Free Markets vs. *Real* Socialism   43

     The Bourgeoisie on "Human Nature" and Religion:
     The Marxist Response   55

     Once Again on Bourgeois Economics
     and Bourgeois Mystification   61

     Who Really Upholds National Liberation,
     And What Internationalism Is Really About   62

     The Dictatorship of the Proletariat:
     A Million Times More Democratic—For the *Masses*   65

     Communism Is Not a "Utopian Tyranny,"
     But a Realizable and Liberating Goal   68

Mechanical "Historical Materialism" and
Dialectical Historical Materialism   73

Chapter 2
Once Again on the Historical Experience of the Proletarian Revolution—Once More on Conquering the World   79

The Question of Productive Forces   80

The World Revolution: Advance and Consolidation   82

Proletarian Revolution and Internationalism—
The Social Base   85

Grasp Revolution, Promote Production   87

    Transforming Relations Among People—
    and Transforming Ownership   87

    Egalitarianism and Common Abundance
    Under Socialism   93

    What Does It Mean for the Masses
    To Be Masters of Society?   96

    Socialist Construction in the World Context   99

Conclusion: The Ideological Confrontation   107

Two World Outlooks—Two Opposing Views of Freedom   108

Moving Beyond Bourgeois Right   114

Technology—and Ideology   117

Changing Society, Changing "Human Nature"   119

Historical Materialism and Making History   120

About Bob Avakian   124

Publisher's Preface

This is a book that upholds revolution and communism. That fact alone marks its significance. For this is a critical historical hour. The international guardians of the status quo are trumpeting the triumph and permanence of capitalism. "Can't you smell the coffee? There is no use fighting for a different kind of world, and you might as well get used to this one." In a thousand different ways we are told that history has judged communism to be a "grand failure," that revolutions inevitably lead to nightmare. This ideological offensive is an undisguised celebration of everything that is vile about capitalism and its vicious New World Order. Yet even among those who are not the celebrants, the message takes its toll—in the lowering of sights, in the narrowing of horizons.

Amidst this barrage and disorientation, Bob Avakian has written a defiant and powerful manifesto. No, this is not the best of all possible worlds but a cruel and outmoded global system that cries out for deep-going change. Yes, there is a liberating and practical alternative to a social order based on competitiveness, greed, and social division. And far from being that radical alternative, the system that collapsed in the Soviet Union was a counterfeit socialism whose oppressive economic and political structures were those of capitalism.

This book is addressed to a broad audience. To the millions in the ghettos and barrios, in the housing projects and prisons, who yearn to be free of exploitation and the daily degradation and horror that is this system. To those itching to get it on with these

i

world-class oppressors, and who want the science to be able to do so. To rebel youth checking out different philosophies and ideologies. To veterans of various revolutionary struggles and movements trying to sort through the lessons of recent history. To those who refuse to give up their dreams of liberation but who are confused by the political earthquakes of the last few years. To the newly awakened and outraged who want to know how to end poverty, racism, war, and the very destruction of the earth; who want to know the truth about and relevance of revolutionary communism.

The collapse of the former Soviet bloc has raised big questions in the minds of many who have been committed to revolutionary change and socialism. Why is it that genuine socialist revolutions have gone sour, with more than a few of their leaders corrupted? Have the theoretical and organizational foundations of socialist revolution as practiced in this century been fundamentally flawed? Are the historic goals and methods of socialism still valid, or must socialism be "reinvented"? This questioning and debate are also part of the backdrop of this book and the theoretical work that has engaged Bob Avakian over the last few years. And these are hardly academic matters. Because the struggle to defend and define a revolutionary vision, and to correctly evaluate the advances and setbacks along the road of bringing classless society into being, is completely bound up with the struggle to forge ahead in the current situation.

This book has a twofold purpose. First, it answers head-on some of the most immediate and cherished charges leveled against communism. These run the gamut—from arguments about human nature being incompatible with socialist values, to misrepresentations of how planned economies work, to claims that communism is a form of modern tyranny. Second, the book grapples with larger, more world-historic questions that have been thrown up by the experience of revolution and counterrevolution in this century. Tough and knotty questions involving such core issues as the defense and spread of proletarian revolutions in a world dominated by imperialism; or how the struggle to create a new society can change not just economic structures but also people, and how the basic people can in fact become the rulers. Avakian approaches these questions both with historical sweep and with an eye to the current state and demands of the world. Here, as in previous studies, Avakian the visionary shines through: he shows the communist revolution to be an epochal transformation of property relations and ideas that touches the most fundamental aspects and patterns of human existence.

At the same time that this book is being published, *A World to Win* magazine is publishing a special issue containing a major essay by Bob Avakian entitled "Democracy: More Than Ever We Can And Must Do Better Than That." That essay answers arguments put forward by the Central Reorganisation Committee, Communist Party of India (Marxist-Leninist) and expands upon some of the themes of this book. In particular, it examines and assesses the basic historical experience of the dictatorship of the proletariat and the leading role of a communist party. The way the question basically poses itself is this: Are such forms obstacles or necessities for the proletariat, and ultimately all humanity, in achieving liberation? Avakian argues that the experience of proletarian revolution since Marx, including the contributions of Lenin and Mao, has been basically right on these questions.

Taken together that essay and this book form a two-volume work. It adds up to a spirited defense and presentation of revolutionary communism, of the capacity of Marxism to confront the most complex and burning issues that face humanity at the dawn of the twenty-first century, and of the necessity and possibility to advance human society beyond its present foundations of commodity production, exploitation, and social fragmentation. And in summing up the proletariat's historical experience in creating a new world—both the achievements and the mistakes—Bob Avakian points to key lessons for the next wave of revolution. Which is after all the point. To understand the world in order to change it. More so than ever.

Introduction

Two major events in recent times have had significant worldwide effects: the victory of U.S. imperialism and its "coalition" in its war against Iraq; and the coup/countercoup events in the Soviet Union in the summer of 1991, which resulted in what the world powers and their media insist on calling the "defeat"—and they insist it is the "final" or all-but-final defeat—of "communism."

These two events are, of course, objectively related to each other. The overwhelming victory for U.S. imperialism and its "coalition" in the Persian Gulf war would not have been possible if it weren't for the changes that had already taken place within the Soviet Union and in its role in the world, even before the more recent coup/countercoup events. And, at the same time, this overwhelming military victory for U.S. imperialism in many ways sharpened the contradictions within the ruling circles of the Soviet Union and played a role in bringing those contradictions to a head.

But beyond that, the imperialists—and the U.S. imperialists in particular—have seized on these events and tied them together in an intensified propaganda offensive aimed at impressing on both rival powers of various kinds and the masses of people throughout the world that these imperialists are all-powerful. That there is no real possibility of really standing up to them and defeating them militarily. And furthermore that there is no real alternative to their system anyway—that this is after all the best possible, or only possible, "way of life" and that any attempt to replace this with something radically different—in particular communism—is bound to end in disaster. Therefore the only thing to do is to accept the world as it is—as it is dictated from above—and at most to aspire to climb higher within the confines of this system. Over and over this message is blared, in triumphal tones, through all the media and mouthpieces of the ruling powers.

We cannot say that this is having no effect. It is affecting the morale and the vision of the people, including the masses of proletarians and other oppressed people. It is, of course, not extinguishing the hatred of these masses for the reality of what this system means for them—the hardship, suffering, exploitation, oppression, and degradation that it means for them daily, hourly, and continually. Nor can it prevent their anger from continually bursting out into protest and rebellion of many different kinds. But it is influencing these spontaneous struggles of the masses—as well as the outlook of more organized forces involved in these struggles. It is influencing both the way in which people fight and, even more fundamentally, the goals for which they are fighting—what changes they demand, what changes they see as both desirable and possible. It is tending to narrow and restrict people's vision to the terms and limits of the new *old* world order.

This is also having a real effect within the ranks of the conscious revolutionary forces, including within the international communist movement, among those who have upheld the line of Mao Tsetung and, as an important part of that, have long recognized that the Soviet Union itself for many decades was no longer socialist but had become *social-imperialist*—socialist in words and in outer appearance but imperialist in fact and in deed.

The situation today is in some important ways similar to the one that Lenin wrote about in "The Collapse of the Second International." There is an irony in this because the situation then was one of world war (the first world war), whereas today's situation is one that has come about, to a significant degree, because world war has been avoided in the present period, largely as a result of the changes associated with the regime of Mikhail Gorbachev (and now increasingly Boris Yeltsin). But still the world today is one marked by great upheaval, sudden and dramatic changes, and underlying crisis that is by no means resolved or fundamentally "under control."

Writing about the collapse of the Second (Socialist) International into opportunism after the outbreak of World War 1, Lenin made the observation that "the experience of the war, like the experience of any crisis in history, of any great calamity and any sudden turn in human life, stuns and breaks some people, *but enlightens and tempers others*" ("The Collapse of the Second International," Lenin, *Collected Works [LCW]*, Moscow, Progress Publishers, v. 21, p. 216). And he pointed out that one of the distinguishing features of those socialists who were stunned and broken by the experience of the war was that even before then, they had begun to adopt an evolutionary orientation in place of a revolutionary one and were unprepared for suddenly erupting radical changes of one kind or another. Such people, Lenin said, are characterized by "a fear of sharp turns and a disbelief in them" (p. 243).

A radically different response is required—the current situation must be radically transformed. And here again is another one of those "more than ever" truths: It is the revolutionary communists who can and must lead the way in doing this: those who continue to stand on the basis of Marxism-Leninism-Maoism and to grasp that in fact only by applying the principles of Marxism-Leninism-Maoism is it possible not only to maintain your bearings but to advance in the face of the current world situation. This is our duty and our challenge. But we can do this only by recognizing, directly confronting, and grappling deeply with the basic and profound questions that have been thrown up by the present situation. This is a matter of applying materialist dialectics: grasping the positive as well as the negative aspects of the situation; recognizing not only the immediate difficulties created by this situation but even more the fact that overall and strategically the world situation has grown more favorable for proletarian revolution; seizing hold of the positive factors and, through struggle, turning a bad thing into a good thing, as Mao put it.

In the final analysis and overall, the answer to the ideological offensive of the powers-that-be and the solution to the problems confronting the masses of people must be given in the material world—in the realm of politics and ultimately the highest form of politics—the all-out military struggle for political power in society.

Here the example of the revolution in Peru stands out. This is a revolutionary people's war led by the Communist Party of Peru, a party upholding the banner of Marxism-Leninism-Maoism and applying it concretely in practice in the revolutionary struggle of the people to transform that society and, as the Peruvian comrades say, to serve the world revolution. This gives what Lenin described as "the dignity of immediate actuality" to Maoist revolution: it shows in practice the profound truth and power of Marxism-Leninism-Maoism.* And this is a very positive factor of real and growing significance in today's world situation.

At the same time, there is the underlying fact that, even with their overwhelming military victory in the Persian Gulf war, with the world-shaking events in the (former) Soviet Union and what had been its bloc, and with the political-ideological offensive the imperialists have launched in connection with these events—even with all that, and despite all their triumphal declarations, they have not been able to solve the crisis in which the imperialist system is enmeshed.

First of all, the situation in the U.S. itself is marked by serious problems with the economy, deep faultlines, sharp polarization, repeated rebellion and upheavals, and the potential for this on a

---

* In "On Practice" Mao quoted Lenin's summation that *"Practice is higher than (theoretical) knowledge,* for it has not only the dignity of universality, but also of immediate actuality" (Mao Tsetung, *Selected Works [SW]*, Peking, Foreign Languages Press (FLP), v. 1., p. 297).

far grander scale.* And similar kinds of contradictions exist throughout the capitalist-imperialist world. This is true not only in the countries formerly in the Soviet bloc, where today social contradictions of various kinds are finding explosive expression; it is also true in the Western imperialist countries as well.

Furthermore, there are many contradictions among the imperialists themselves, and although some of these have been mitigated by the changes in the Soviet Union and its role in the world, others are beginning to surface more prominently—such as that between Germany and others in the Western bloc, including the U.S.; those between Japan and the U.S.; and others—and these contradictions are likely to become even more pronounced in the period ahead. Also, the contradictions between the Soviet Union (or the new state that is replacing it) and other imperialists are still a significant factor in the world, even while these contradictions are undergoing substantial changes. The point is not that the threat of world war is now posing itself in the same way—and with the same acuteness and immediacy—that it did in the first half of the 1980s; but conflicts of various kinds among the imperialists are real and are bound to make themselves felt. All is not and cannot be "one big happy family" among these imperialists; if they can be compared to a family, it is much more a mafia "family."

The situation in the Third World countries is one of ongoing economic crisis, sharply expressing itself in terms of a massive debt crisis and growing poverty and immiseration of the already miserable masses, the remaining explosiveness of many regions and instability of many regimes, and so on.

In all this—in considering the situation and events in the U.S. and other capitalist-imperialist countries as well as in the oppressed nations of the Third World—it is very important to keep in mind the contradiction between what this system promises and what it delivers. This is related to Marx's famous statement that

* I won't repeat here but refer the reader to the characterization of the situation of U.S. imperialism, including within its own homeland, which was made in the beginning sections of "The End of a Stage—Beginning of a New Stage," *Revolution*, Fall 1990: the analysis there continues to correctly characterize the situation of U.S. imperialism today.

the important thing at any given time is not what the masses understand or are doing but what they will be compelled to do by the workings of the system itself. The system will be the system—it will act and treat the masses of people according to its own inner dynamics and "logic"—it will exploit and oppress the masses of people under its rule. And, as Mao Tsetung said, where there is oppression, there is resistance.

At the same time, while it remains very true and very important that, overall and in the final analysis, the answer to the powers-that-be and their ideological offensive must be delivered in the material sphere, right now especially it is also very important to take them on in the ideological realm itself. In fact, this is a key part of building the struggle toward the goal of defeating them in the material sphere—of seizing power. The recent events which these imperialists have leaped to declare "the death of communism"—and the very fact that these imperialists have focused popular attention on the question of communism and made it a "mass question"—all this gives heightened importance and urgency to *our* ideological counteroffensive, even as we continue to wage the battle against them in the material sphere as the most decisive battle—that is, political struggle, assuming its highest form of military struggle when the conditions for this exist or emerge.

It is this ideological struggle—and particularly the questions that have been brought forward in even sharper terms by the recent events in the world, particularly those in the Soviet Union—that I want to speak to here.

This involves both answering some of the more immediate arguments thrown up by the representatives of the new old world order and grappling with larger, more world-historic questions concerning the proletarian revolution and the goal of communism. And there is an interconnection here: these world-historic questions themselves must be repeatedly returned to and wrangled with from different angles in relation to current world events and to the declarations and distortions of the imperialists concerning these events and their larger meaning.

To a large degree, this is focused around the experience of the

Soviet Union since the time of the October 1917 proletarian revolution led by Lenin and the Bolsheviks, but it also involves questions more broadly concerning the experience of socialist revolutions—in particular the Chinese revolution—and of the international communist movement overall.

Although the talk "The End of a Stage—The Beginning of a New Stage" was given before the coup/countercoup events in the Soviet Union, I believe those events and the changes that have accompanied them and flowed from them have confirmed and further underscored the analysis made in that talk—both its analysis of the character of the changes in the Soviet Union in this present period and of how this fits into the larger process of proletarian revolution and bourgeois counterrevolution in this whole historical era. And certainly recent world events have emphasized the importance of the orientation (indicated in the title) of the talk "Mao More Than Ever," published together with "End/Beginning." So, again, what I want to speak to here—with those two talks serving as a kind of background and framework—are certain questions that have been brought more sharply to the fore by major world events in the time since those two talks were published, only a little more than a year ago.

1.

The "Demise of Communism"— and the Communist Future

In reality, what we are witnessing in (what was) the Soviet Union is the further dismantling of the apparatus and institutions of *social* imperialism and their replacement by more and more openly "old-style" bourgeois rule and imperialism. In fact, the recent events make even clearer what was said in "End/ Beginning":

> "The so-called 'demise of communism' is really just revisionism becoming more *openly* bourgeois. This does not constitute a 'crisis' for genuine communism and it is not a bad thing for us—for the international proletariat and the international communist movement, as represented specifically by the RIM [Revolutionary Internationalist Movement] and the parties and organizations affiliated with it. Strategically, it is a fine thing for us." (*Revolution*, #60, Fall 1990, p. 9)

Still, there is a need to dig into this more deeply and specifically to answer some of the main arguments now being made about

9

how this represents the death of communism, its historical failure. Again, the two talks, "End/Beginning" and "Mao More Than Ever," and in a broader sense the overall line of our Party and indeed the whole of Marxism-Leninism-Maoism, have already refuted these arguments, but it is worthwhile to respond to them here directly.

First, an overall point: it is very important to grasp and to insist on the fundamental distinction between *failure* and *defeat* in terms of what has happened with the experience of proletarian revolution so far. We are in a situation where once again there are no longer any socialist countries in the world, for the time being; but this must be viewed in the context of the whole historical process of proletarian revolution and the profound difference between this and all previous revolutions in history.

As pointed out in "End/Beginning," while even the greatest leaders of the international proletariat, such as Lenin and Mao, have of course made mistakes, the loss in China, like the loss in the Soviet Union before it, was not primarily the result of the mistakes of revolutionaries. Still less is it a question of some inherent "defect" in communism and proletarian revolution. Rather, it was primarily a defeat inflicted by the international bourgeoisie. And it is important to recall here the point made in "End/Beginning" about how, after all, the bourgeoisie in its rise to power took several centuries before it was able to firmly imprint its stamp on society and firmly recast society in its image, that is, as a capitalist society. Along the way it was forced to go through many twists and turns and suffered a number of setbacks.

We should hardly expect that the proletarian revolution will have it easier or go through less twists and turns, and reversals and setbacks, before it reaches final victory. After all, as compared with all of these previous revolutions in which one class overthrew another, proletarian revolution seeks to make those two radical ruptures of which Marx and Engels spoke: the radical rupture with traditional property relations and with traditional ideas. It seeks not to replace one form of exploitation with another but to do away with all forms of exploitation and indeed ultimately to eliminate all class distinctions. So, for this very reason, we can only expect and must be prepared for the fact that the proletarian revolution will be even more tortuous than previous revolutions; will undergo a longer, more complex process of revolution and counterrevolution before it reaches its final goal of communism worldwide.

With this historical perspective and with a sober, scientific analysis of present-day reality, we can take on directly the claim that Marxism has been defeated and communism is dead. Marxism, with its demonstration of the possibility and necessity of communist revolution, is continuously vindicated by reality, *including recent world events*; and today, with its development into Marxism-Leninism-Maoism, it represents, more than ever, the wave of the future.

The Three Milestones

In order to demonstrate this in its fullest and deepest dimension, it is worthwhile to begin by reviewing what we can call the three milestones of Marxism-Leninism-Maoism. That is, the contributions—the historic breakthroughs—that were made by Marx and then, in turn, Lenin and Mao, which represented qualitative leaps in the development of a comprehensive scientific understanding of reality and of the means of transforming it through revolutionary struggle.

MARX

It was Marx who, over 100 years ago, first forged and systematized this understanding on a fundamental level. The theoretical and methodological foundation for this—the outlook and methodology that Marx, more than anyone else, synthesized—is the basic philosophical outlook of Marxism: dialectical materialism and historical materialism (the application of dialectical materialism to human society and its development). In this necessarily brief summation of the development of Marxism into Marxism-Leninism-Maoism, I am not going to attempt to elaborate on the philosophical-methodological principles of dialectical materialism but will focus on their application to human society and its development and their application to the revolutionary struggle as expressed in revolutionary strategy.

In a very important sense, historical materialism can be considered the pivotal point in Marxism. How is this so and what is the importance of historical materialism?

Historical Materialism— The Pivotal Point of Marxism

Briefly, Marx brought into focus, out of all the confusion that had surrounded all attempts to understand history up to that time, the fundamental underlying reality of human existence—that, in order for human beings to survive and continue in existence from generation to generation, it is necessary for them to produce and reproduce the material requirements of life. On one level this seems obvious, and Marx was naturally not the first to recognize this necessity as such. But it was only with Marxism that this was understood to be the foundation and point of departure for an understanding of human society and its historical development. But that is not all: of equally fundamental importance is the fact that, in order to produce and reproduce the material requirements of life—in order to carry out production and exchange—people have to enter into very definite social relations, most fundamentally, production relations.

Production does not and cannot get carried out in the abstract. It doesn't get carried out in some sort of formless way, or by people just entering arbitrarily into relations which they can choose and change at will. It is carried out, of necessity, through very definite relations between people in production. And, in turn, these production relations are determined by the level and character of the productive forces that are at hand at any given time in society. Productive forces, to put it simply, refers to the means of production (the tools and instruments that are used in production, including land and raw materials) and the people themselves with their knowledge and abilities in terms of using these means of production and carrying out production generally.

That the character of the production relations is determined by the character of the productive forces is true regardless of whether the tools and instruments at hand are the very early tools, the simple tools of early human existence, or the most developed machinery and technology of the present age. For example, try to imagine the production relations of the capitalist factory system being applied in a simple agricultural community where there is no modern machinery or modern means of transportation and communication! And in the future, when technology has again leaped far beyond what we know (or even imagine) today, while the production relations then will be radically different, the principle will remain in effect: the production and social relations of society will be founded upon and generally correspond to the character and level of development of the productive forces.

Marx identified the production relations of society (arising on the basis of given productive forces) as the economic base of society. Further, Marx showed that on the foundation of this economic base there arise certain political institutions, laws, customs, etc., as well as certain ways of thinking, culture, and so on. And these, constituting the political/ideological superstructure of society, not only have their origin in the economic base but also ultimately correspond to the character of that economic base—the way in which people come together in order to produce and reproduce the material requirements of life.

Any time production or the economy is discussed, the first thing that must be asked and determined is: what are the underlying *production relations*—which, in class society, means the *class relations*—through which that production is carried out, and what is the nature of the superstructure corresponding to those underlying economic relations? Any other way of approaching this is misguided and misleading.

What is more, proceeding from the understanding that the productive forces are not static but dynamic—that, because of the very nature of human beings and their society, people are continually developing the productive forces and bringing forward new productive forces—Marx brought to light how, at a certain point in the development of the productive forces, they will come into antagonistic conflict with the existing production relations, which are based on previous productive forces. What becomes clear at such times is that the existing production relations have ceased to be the most appropriate form for the development of the productive forces and have turned into a *fetter* on that development. At that point a social revolution becomes necessary to unleash the productive forces, to bring about a revolutionary transformation in the production relations in order to bring them into conformity with the new productive forces.

This social revolution takes place, and can only take place, in the superstructure of society—specifically in the political arena and, in a concentrated way, in the military struggle for political power over society as a whole. And, from the time that society splits up into different and opposing classes—from the time that production relations involve the separation of people into distinct groups, some of which exploit the others—then society is marked by class struggle, and social revolution takes place through the overthrow of one class by another. At any given time, the class that can organize society in such a way as to make the most rational use of the productive forces—the class which represents relations of production most in correspondence with the productive forces and capable of acting as the most appropriate form for their development—is bound to gain the ruling position in society, although this will happen only through a process of profound class struggle.

Marxism shows how this has applied throughout the history of class society. But Marxism also makes clear that human society has not always been—and will not always be—divided into classes; and it shows how—on what basis, owing to what developments and changes—human society first split into different and antagonistic classes. The earliest human societies are communal societies in which production is carried out by people in common and the division of labor does not involve oppression of one part of the people by another. However, with the development of the productive forces, once enough is produced that surpluses can be privately appropriated by a part of society, even while the majority remain at more or less a subsistence level, then the relations of people in production will assume the character of relations between different social classes, that is, different groups in society which are marked by their differing relationship to the means of production (whether or not they own land, machinery, and other instruments of production and how much of these they own); by their role in the social productive process (their place in society's division of labor); and by their consequent share in the distribution of social wealth.

From the time that society has been divided into classes, the class which at any given time has dominated the production process—which has monopolized ownership of the means of production—has forced the rest of society to labor under its command and in its interests. It has controlled the surplus produced and decided what to do with it—to what degree to use it for personal consumption, to what extent to apply it to maintaining and fortifying the institutions of society, to what extent to reinvest it to further develop the economy. And the class which at any given time has dominated the economic life of society in this way has also dominated all of the rest of society. It has controlled and used the superstructure—in particular the organs of political power: the bureaucracy, the government administration, and above all the military forces that it can maintain out of the surplus it accumulates—to suppress and to keep in an oppressed condition the classes which it exploits, the masses of working people.

Marx also specifically pointed out that whatever was the character of the economically dominant ruling class, such would be the character of the ruling ideas of that age. And this is reflected in religion, the arts, and other spheres of culture, as well as in politics, philosophy, and so on. In other words, through the institutions of society, the ruling class controls the dissemination of ideas and determines which ideas dominate in society. From the time of the emergence of classes, the thinking of different people has in the final analysis basically corresponded to their class position, but at the same time the outlook of everyone in society is strongly influenced by the ideas of the class that dominates the economic base of society and therefore dominates the political/ideological superstructure.

In sum, the superstructure of society will reflect the class relations: it will be controlled by and serve the interests of the economically dominant class...until such time as that class and the relations of production it represents and enforces become an obstacle to the further development of the productive forces, whereupon a class representing new production relations, corresponding to the new character of the productive forces, will lead the people in rising up against the old ruling class and finally overthrowing it, whereupon the rising class seizes political power and reshapes society in accordance with its interests...until such time... This is what Marx (and Engels) meant when they wrote in the "Communist Manifesto" that, from the time of the emergence of classes thousands of years ago, the history of society has been the history of class struggle.

While all of this may be rather elementary to anyone familiar with the basic principles of Marxism, that is only because Marx created the theoretical synthesis bringing all this to light; and this represented a real revolution in human thought, a radical rupture with all previous ways of (mis)understanding the underlying basis and laws of motion of human society. It represented a tremendous historical breakthrough, first of all, to show that there was in fact what Marx described as a "coherence" in human history, because of the fact that each generation inherits the productive forces developed up to that time and in turn further develops them and "passes them on" to the next generation. Even if this involves destruction and then rebuilding, still there is a certain motion to this, with all of its contradiction, that gives this coherence to human history. And this coherence in human history increases, and increasingly involves humanity as a whole, the more the productive forces develop and different peoples all over the globe interact and are bound together through production and exchange.

This understanding explodes the notion that human history is simply a series of accidents, either without any underlying cause or caused by some supernatural beings or forces (gods or some other supernatural forces) and/or by the actions of individuals, particularly "great" individuals (kings, princes, emperors, presidents, heads of big corporations and owners of big slave plantations, and so on), exerting their will on society. It was a great leap to show that this is not how history is made, but that history is made as a result of the struggle between different social groupings—different classes in class society—and that this in turn is rooted in the underlying economic foundation of society, as has been summarized here.

As we know, however, Marx did not merely reveal the coherence in human history nor only bring to light the material basis and motive causes of the emergence of classes and the history of class struggle. Beyond that, he showed where this whole process is heading—that this class struggle will result in the triumph of the proletariat, a class which emerges in capitalist society, on the basis of its socialized productive forces, and which represents not a new way of organizing production in conditions where one class exploits another, but a way of taking advantage of the development of the productive forces so that they are utilized in common and that there is no longer any exploitation and in fact no longer any class divisions.

Marx showed that the proletariat can and must do this because, with the development of capitalism and the corresponding development of the productive forces, the productive forces themselves become highly socialized, that is, they are usable only if they are used in common by thousands and ultimately millions of people. The proletariat is the class which does work in common this way in its thousands and millions. The proletariat is the class which represents socialized production. It represents socialized relations of production—it represents the relations of production that correspond to the most rational utilization of the productive forces, the most appropriate form for the liberation and further development of the productive forces.

But the capitalist class appropriates the results of production as private (capitalist) property, as capital. The capitalist class represents and enforces relations of production that have become shackles on the productive forces as they have developed under the capitalist system itself. It must be overthrown: the system of ownership and appropriation it upholds and all the social relations, institutions and ideas corresponding to this must be abolished, surpassed. And this can only be done by abolishing all forms of exploitation and all division of labor that involves social antagonism. This is the historic task of the proletariat.

In carrying out its social revolution, the proletariat resolves the underlying contradiction of the capitalist system, the contradiction between socialized production and private (capitalist) appropriation. The proletariat, when it has overthrown the political power of the capitalist class and established its own political power, socializes the ownership of the means of production and, through stages, develops them to the point where they become the common property of all of society. At the same time it transforms the political institutions and the ways of thinking of the people, in other words the superstructure, such that eventually classes are eliminated and a whole new kind of human society—a society without class distinctions, without social antagonisms, without oppression of one part of society by another—is brought into being and then in turn further develops under the communist system.

So this is the tremendous breakthrough that Marx made in terms of pointing to the coherence in human history and giving a coherent understanding of human history—in showing its sharply contradictory but understandable development and the fact that through all that development it will eventually reach the stage where the communist revolution will come on the agenda and be carried out. For a succinct summary on this decisive question, we can turn to what Marx himself wrote in 1852:

"...As to myself, no credit is due to me for discovering the existence of classes in modern society, nor yet the struggle between them. Long before me bourgeois historians had described the historical development of this struggle of the classes, and bourgeois economists the economic anatomy of the classes. What I did that was new was to prove: 1) that the *existence of classes* is only bound up with *particular historical phases in the development of production;* 2) that the class struggle necessarily leads to the *dictatorship of the proletariat;* 3) that this dictatorship itself only constitutes the transition to the *abolition of all classes* and to a *classless society....*" (Marx to Joseph Weydemeyer, March 5, 1852, Marx and Engels, *Selected Letters,* Peking, FLP, p. 18)

The Dirty Little Secret
of Capitalist Exploitation

Now, along with this, Marx also analyzed and laid bare the inner workings of the capitalist system itself and particularly what has been called "the dirty little secret of capitalist exploitation." That is, he penetrated beneath the outer appearance of the relationship between the capitalist owners and the workers who labor under the command of the capitalists—a relationship which appears to be one of equality, an equal exchange of wages for work. Marx showed that this relationship, beneath its outer appearance of equality, contains a fundamental relationship of exploitation and oppression.

Marx did this not simply by denouncing the capitalists for being rich and not simply by showing the tremendous discrepancy between the immense wealth controlled by the capitalists and the abject poverty of the masses of workers. He penetrated to the inner essence of how this comes about and he also showed why it is no longer necessary. Capitalism is not only a generalized commodity-producing society where things—or things of real and social importance—are overwhelmingly produced not for immediate use but in order to be sold for a money price; beyond that, capitalism is characterized by the fact that labor power (the ability to work) has itself become a commodity.

As a commodity, labor power has value, the same as all commodities do. The value of this commodity, labor power, is determined in the same way, by the same measure, as all commodities—by the *socially necessary labor time* required to produce that commodity (the labor time actually necessary under the prevailing social conditions of production). This means that the value of the commodity, labor power, is equal to the value of the things (commodities) that are required to keep the workers alive, able to work, and able to produce new generations of workers. While the specific level of development of the productive forces may vary from one capitalist country to another, nevertheless in capitalist society, generally, the value of the commodity labor power is less than the total value produced by the workers during the time they are working for the capitalists. Thus, part of the labor of the workers is paid labor—labor spent producing an amount of value equal to the value of their labor power (corresponding to their wages); but the other part is *unpaid* labor—labor spent producing value for which the workers receive no equivalent in exchange, value which is entirely appropriated by the capitalists.

This is the source, and the only source, of the profit of the capitalists—the source of their personal income but, more than that, the source of their ability to reinvest and expand their capitalist enterprise. It is the source of their ability to control society and finance the institutions, in particular the political and military institutions, which in turn are used to suppress the working class and the masses of people.

Now, in any society where a surplus is produced beyond what people need for mere survival, it will be the case that this surplus will not simply be divided among the people, or else there would be no way for society's productive forces to qualitatively develop, no way to provide for possible natural disasters or other unforeseen developments, no way to provide for the administration of society and for people's educational, cultural, and other needs, and so on. Marx emphasized that this would be true in communist society no less than under capitalism. But he also emphasized the radical difference that, in communist society, the appropriation of the surplus and its allocation for various social needs will be regulated by the people themselves—by a society of freely associated human beings, without class distinctions—just as the process of production itself will be. By contrast, in capitalist society, the production process and the appropriation and allocation of the surplus is controlled by a class standing above and dominating those who produce that surplus—and social wealth as a whole—the working people. The more the workers slave under capitalism the more they strengthen the power of capital, the more they re-create and fortify the conditions of their own enslavement.

In short, Marx showed that the production of value and particularly of *surplus value*—that is, the value created by the workers in producing, as commodities, the products of capitalist society; and within that *the extra value for which the workers get nothing, but which goes to the capitalists*—is the driving force of capitalist accumulation. It is the inner essence of capitalist society, "the dirty little secret of capitalist exploitation," and the basis of the oppression of the proletariat. And, Marx explained, the subordination of the workers to the process of capitalist accumulation reduces them to a situation where they can live only so long as they can work, and they can work only so long as a capitalist can make sufficient profit by exploiting them. Thus, at one and the same time, capitalism results in and depends upon the ruthless exploitation of the workers who are employed and the existence of workers who are unemployed—a "reserve army of labor" whose ranks swell to huge numbers in times of economic crisis under capitalism.

Thus, Marx showed that, while the workers must fight to keep from being crushed and broken under the capitalist system, no struggle that is limited to the demand for the improvement of their conditions within the capitalist system can fundamentally alter the situation of the working class: only by rising up, recognizing its higher interest as a class, overthrowing the capitalist system, and moving on to carry out the communist transformation of society can the working class fundamentally change its own condition and that of humanity as a whole.

In his development and application of historical materialism, Marx (together with Engels) had brought to light how the emergence of relations of exploitation and oppression—including, as one of the most fundamental aspects of this, the emergence of social conditions that resulted in the oppression of women—was bound up with the development of class divisions, which in turn was bound up with certain phases of the development of production. Marx went on to show how capitalism represents the last of these phases of production—the last form of human society in which class division and social antagonisms will exist—and how the proletariat, through its revolutionary overthrow of capitalism and radical transformation of society, will abolish all forms of exploitation and oppression and all class distinctions.

At the same time, Marx emphasized and explained why the proletariat, as opposed to all other classes in contemporary society and indeed in history, must have internationalism as its outlook, as opposed to nationalism. Even though in the bourgeois era the world is divided into different nations, the proletariat is an international class and its interests, as a class, lie in achieving communism worldwide. Indeed, communism can only be achieved on a worldwide basis—by eliminating relations of exploitation and social antagonism, oppression and inequality, throughout the globe.

That internationalism is the outlook and the political stand of the proletariat is based on a fundamental reality, the reality of the capitalist system itself as a world system of commodity production and of exploitation. A system which requires and necessitates and increasingly draws together a world market and subordinates it to the domination of capital; and which, particularly in its imperialist stage (as will be discussed shortly), integrates the entire world economy into its process of accumulation, though this involves many different particular systems of production and countries at different levels of development. Thus Marx showed that internationalism must be the outlook of the proletariat and that, as Marx put it, only by emancipating all mankind could the proletariat emancipate itself.

And, just as Marx exposed the inner essence of the relationship between the capitalists and the workers (between the bourgeoisie and the proletariat) within capitalist society itself, he also exposed the plunder and colonial depredations of England and other major capitalist countries in India, Egypt, China, and all over the world. As Marx summarized, with powerful sweep and irony:

> "The discovery of gold and silver in America, the extirpation, enslavement and entombment in mines of the aboriginal population, the beginning of the conquest and looting of the East Indies, the turning of Africa into a warren for the commercial hunting of black-skins, signalized the rosy dawn of the era of capitalist production." (Marx, *Capital*, New York, International Publishers, 1970, v. 1., p. 751)

Marx revealed not only how all of this was inseparably linked with capitalism, but, moreover, how the proletarian revolution would finally put an end to all of this, on a worldwide basis. And, as a practical expression of this, Marx (together with Engels) was in the leadership in the founding of the first international organization of workers from different countries, known as the First International.

Here we must stop and ask, are these fundamental principles of communism and the outlook and methodology that are their foundation—are these in any way "disproved by reality" or "outdated"? Do events in the world, do facts, do the daily experiences of the masses of people not only in one country, including in the U.S., but all over the world—does all this show that these principles are not valid or not relevant? Do these principles no longer correspond to accurate descriptions or analysis of the daily occurrences and still more the inner essence and workings of the capitalist system and its relations within countries and internationally?

In no way—just the opposite! These principles of communism not only remain valid, but are more than ever the basis for piercing the fog of distortion spread by the spokesmen for the old order and grasping what is really going on in the world. They are the basis for correctly understanding and radically transforming the world in the interests of the masses of people and ultimately humanity as a whole.

But Marxism is a living science and continues to develop with the development of, and with changes in, reality, including in human society. This leads to the discussion of the second great milestone of Marxism, which is Leninism.

LENIN

More or less at the end of the 19th century, capitalism developed into imperialism, and it was Lenin who analyzed this and showed its implications for the proletarian revolution worldwide. Examining the new features of capitalism in its imperialist stage, Lenin showed how it had become even more an international system of accumulation—and of exploitation as the basis of that accumulation.*

---

* In the following summary on imperialism, I have drawn from Lenin's *Imperialism, The Highest Stage of Capitalism* and also from *America in Decline*, by Raymond Lotta with Frank Shannon, Chicago, Banner Press, v. 1, particularly the first chapter, "Political Economy in the Epoch of Imperialism and Proletarian Revolution."

Political Economy of Imperialism

Lenin showed how imperialism was distinguished by the growth and dominance of monopoly capital, as opposed to smaller units of capital. Monopoly capital does not necessarily mean literally the domination by one single unit of capital over an entire industry (nor, still less, over the whole economy) but the domination by a few very large and powerful units of capital over whole industries, over whole branches of the economy. And monopoly in this sense is one of the most essential features of capitalism as it developed into its imperialist stage (in fact, while analyzing other essential features of imperialism, Lenin said that, as a shorthand description, imperialism could be equated with monopoly capitalism).

Together with this was the development of finance capital, that is, the merging of industrial and banking capital to form concentrations of tremendous amounts of capital that not only control whole sections of the economy in a particular country but are capable of exerting a major influence on the economies of whole countries, whole regions, even the world economy as a whole. Finance capital is capital that is not necessarily grounded in—its investment is not almost completely bound up with—a particular enterprise or branch of the economy. Rather, it is capital which can be shifted quickly and on a massive scale from one industry, branch of the economy, region, or country, to another. It is capital drawn from many different sources, and while at any given time there are identifiable formations of finance capital and groups of finance capitalists, these are not highly stable and unchanging but, on the contrary, constantly shifting, breaking apart, regrouping in new formations and alliances, not only within particular countries but on an international scale. Again, all this has been made possible by the development of monopoly capital and the merging of bank and industrial capital, creating a situation where literally billions and billions of dollars (yen, marks, francs, rubles, pounds) are controlled and utilized in this way by a very small number of people who are more and more divorced from production, from the actual process through which this value is created. From this it can be seen why Lenin emphasized the *parasitism* of capitalism in its imperialist stage.

Another of the other major characteristics of capitalism that Lenin analyzed was that, with the development of capitalism into imperialism, the export of capital (in the form of direct investments in other countries or in the form of loans or similar financial arrangements) replaced the export of commodities (trade) as the most essential international economic activity of capital. Trade continued to play a very important role, but international investment and other forms of the export of capital came to play an even more decisive part in the overall process of capitalist accumulation, worldwide.

Yet, while the development of capitalism into imperialism meant that there was a further leap in the internationalization of capital and the enmeshing of all parts of the world and various different systems of production into an overall process of capitalist accumulation on a world scale; at the same time, capital, which had arisen fundamentally on the basis of the national market in the various capitalist countries, remained rooted in those national markets. Capital retained its "national identity," even as it accumulated, and could only accumulate, on an international scale. Just as imperialism turned certain features of capitalist commodity production into their opposites yet did not and could not separate itself from its foundation in that commodity production; so imperialism, in certain important respects, leaped beyond the previous relation between the capitalist national market and the world market, yet it did not and could not separate itself from its foundation in that national market. In the imperialist era, the competition among capitals is heightened and that competition finds its most concentrated expression in the contention among imperialist states.

Imperialism, then, means heightened rivalry among especially the large-scale capitalists and, above all, rivalry among the imperialist states for colonial possessions, "spheres of influence," and so on. By the end of the 19th century, this grabbing of colonial possessions and carving up of the world as a whole had been more or less completed; but, given the inner compulsion of capital to expand, along with the particular features of capital in its im-

perialist stage, this meant, and could only have meant, an intensified struggle among the imperialists to redivide what they had
already divided among themselves.

Sooner or later, and repeatedly, this rivalry is bound to assume
the form of warfare among the imperialists—often in an indirect
form ("proxy wars," etc.) and at certain times in direct military
confrontation with each other (generally in the form of war between military alliances, or blocs, each headed by one or a few
powerful imperialist states). But, regardless of the specific outcome of any particular war—even including the all-out wars between imperialist blocs—the inner dynamic of imperialism will
continually create a situation in which such wars will break out
anew. Alliances and truces among the imperialists can never be
permanent and absolute—they are bound to break up, wars of
various kinds are bound to break out, repeatedly. This Lenin
showed through analysis of the essential features of imperialism—
and certainly the whole history of the imperialist era in this century has dramatically demonstrated this and confirmed Lenin's
analysis.

But more than analyzing these new features of imperialism and
laying bare their underlying causes, Lenin showed how this
heightened the possibilities of revolution, in particular the proletarian revolution. And he showed that this revolution need not
occur first in the most advanced countries (technologically) but
could occur first in a more backward country, and it was likely to
occur where, at any given time, the contradictions of the world
imperialist system, interacting with the situation in particular
countries, led to a revolutionary crisis, weakening the ruling class
and heightening the discontent and struggle of the masses.

At the same time, with regard to the advanced capitalist
countries, the development of capitalism into imperialism meant
that the ruling class in all the major imperialist countries was able
to bribe a section of the working class from the spoils of its international exploitation and plunder. This resulted in a split in the
working class, with its more privileged, bribed sections the basis
for, at best, reformist politics, while its basic, most exploited sections remained the social base for proletarian revolution and

proletarian internationalism. Lenin insisted that, in terms of fundamental orientation and strategy, it was necessary to go down lower and deeper to these basic sections of the proletariat in order to maintain a revolutionary line and build a party and movement that could realize the revolutionary aims of the proletariat as a class.

The Vanguard Party of the Proletariat

Lenin not only made these decisive breakthroughs in the development of Marxist theory and its application to the epoch of imperialism, he also took the lead in giving them the "dignity of immediate actuality" as well as universality. In short, through his leadership of the proletarian revolution in Russia and the Soviet Republic it gave birth to, he demonstrated in practice the truth and power of these principles of Marxism-Leninism. He led the proletariat in making the historic breakthrough of not only overthrowing the old order and seizing power but then consolidating that power and embarking upon the socialist transformation of society.

All of this is closely linked to the further development by Lenin of the Marxist understanding of the relationship between consciousness and spontaneity and between vanguard leadership and the masses (between the party and the class and masses it leads). Lenin showed how the consciousness that is developed by the workers spontaneously cannot yet be communist consciousness. "Spontaneous" consciousness, in a society divided into classes and dominated by an exploiting class, is bound to be conditioned by the ideas of the ruling class. In order to rupture with this outlook and develop genuine working class consciousness, Lenin explained, the workers must not confine their concerns and struggles solely or even mainly to the economic struggle (the fight for better wages, working conditions, etc.) but must take up an all-around struggle against the capitalist system and its oppression not only of the workers but of all strata and groups in society.

The workers must concern themselves with every sphere of society and must learn to distinguish the class interests involved in every major social question and world event. Only in this way can they come to grasp the essential nature of the enemy—the capitalist system and its ruling class—and to recognize both the possibility of winning allies among other forces in society *and* the limitations of such allies owing to their class position and outlook. Only in this way can the proletariat become fully conscious of its own class interests and outlook and develop the ability to lead the masses of oppressed people in a struggle determined and powerful enough to carry out the overthrow of the existing system and the establishment of a new, socialist system under the rule of the proletariat.

Along with this, Lenin showed that the development of revolutionary class-consciousness and the waging of a revolutionary struggle by the working class could not happen without the leadership of a vanguard party representing, in a concentrated way, the outlook and interests of the proletariat and fusing this with the struggle of the masses to transform their spontaneous struggle and consciousness into a revolutionary movement guided by communist ideology. This vanguard party should draw its members not only from the proletariat but also from revolutionary-minded people among the intellectuals and other strata in society, but they must all be united on the basis of taking up the stand and viewpoint of the proletariat and wholeheartedly devoting their lives to its emancipatory goals.

The party, if it is to play such a vanguard revolutionary role, cannot be a loose confederation of people united only by their general sympathies with the socialist cause or simply their active involvement in practical struggles of the workers—both of these are important but they are not sufficient. The party must be a highly organized and disciplined organization united on the basis of a common communist outlook and political program. The party must be capable of withstanding the repression of the ruling class and its state apparatus in order to lead, and as part of leading, the masses in rising up against and overthrowing this state power. The party must be structured and function so that it has a unified will and is united in action; it must combine democracy with centralism; it must be characterized by struggle throughout its ranks, on all levels, from bottom to top, to arrive at lines and policies and to select and supervise leaders; and it must operate as a cohesive force, with lower levels voluntarily subordinating themselves to higher levels, particularly in the carrying out of lines and policies. It must have a backbone of full-time professional revolutionaries, and all its members must be characterized by selfless dedication to the revolutionary struggle of the proletariat and to the party in leading that struggle.

It should be clear that, in stressing the importance of vanguard leadership and the role of this vanguard in bringing communist consciousness to the workers, Lenin did not pose this against the fundamental principle that Marx had set forth, that the emancipation of the workers must be won by the workers themselves and cannot be achieved by any group or force substituting itself for the masses. In fact, Lenin showed how the playing of this vanguard role by the communist party strengthens the conscious activism of the masses and is of decisive importance in enabling them to carry out the proletarian revolution.

This was a tremendous breakthrough: before Lenin there had not been as clear an understanding on this question; and, correspondingly, there had not been the development of a highly organized and disciplined party playing this kind of political and ideological vanguard role and *on that basis* relying on the masses and bringing them forward to carry out the revolution. And it is hardly accidental or coincidental that this great contribution by Lenin to the theory and practice of proletarian revolution has been bitterly opposed and attacked by all those who, in one form or another—openly as upholders of the old order or under the banner of one or another kind of reformist "socialism"—oppose the proletarian revolution.

The Further Development of Proletarian Revolution as a World Revolutionary Process

We have seen how Lenin's analysis of imperialism and its implications, politically as well as economically, was decisive in terms of strategic orientation for the proletarian revolution worldwide as well as within particular countries. And an especially important aspect of this was proletarian internationalism: the basis for this internationalism was strengthened both by the objective development of capitalism into imperialism and by Lenin's analysis of this and its strategic implications.

This was concentrated in the stand that Lenin took, and that he led the Bolshevik Party in taking, in relation to World War 1. Before that war, in the period immediately preceding it, the overwhelming majority of parties which had called themselves socialist or communist had pledged themselves to take the stand of opposing the imperialist war with civil war. That is, they had taken the stand of recognizing that the war they could see was about to break out among the imperialists was a war for plunder and exploitation, a war among slavemasters, in which the working class of the various countries had no interest; and that, rather than rallying to the "defense of the fatherland" in this imperialist war, they must lead the masses to struggle against this war and "their own" ruling class and to build this struggle toward the goal of overthrowing this ruling class.

Yet, when this war actually broke out, overwhelmingly these parties threw down the banner of proletarian internationalism and scurried to take up the banner of "the fatherland"—that is, the banner of the imperialists of their own country—against the proletarians and oppressed people of other countries. This was a disgrace and a debacle for the Second International to which these parties adhered. Lenin and the Bolsheviks stood out, if not literally alone, then certainly in the vanguard internationally of those who held firmly to the stand of proletarian internationalism and specifically of "revolutionary defeatism" —that is, working for the defeat of your own imperialist bourgeoisie, welcoming every setback it suffers in the war, and directing all your work toward the goal of turning the imperialist war into a civil war that would overthrow the ruling class and move society forward to socialism.

This is exactly what was done in carrying out the proletarian revolution in Russia right in the midst of World War 1. This was a tremendous contribution in practice, a tremendously powerful demonstration of the principle of proletarian internationalism and its heightened importance in the era of imperialism, as analyzed by Lenin.

The October Revolution and the development of the new Soviet Republic was itself internationalist and made a great contribution to internationalism in two major ways. First, this revolution transformed the old Tsarist empire—which had been called, and rightly so, "the prison-house of nations"—into a real union of peoples, on the basis of equality, under the rule of the proletariat. To grasp the historic significance of this, all we have to do is contrast the tremendous unity between the different nationalities that was achieved through the Soviet revolution with what is erupting today in terms of the outbreaks of bloody conflict, under reactionary leadership, between different nationalities in the (former) Soviet Union and the contest among the bourgeoisies of these nationalities for domination over the others. This is another expression of the fact that, under the rule of the social-imperialists since the time of Khrushchev, the Soviet Union has once more become a "prison-house of nations." Now the adoption of open forms of bourgeois rule and capitalism has been accompanied by the open eruption of these national antagonisms, but this is bitter fruit whose roots lie in the rise to power of revisionism and the reversion of the Soviet Union from socialism to social-imperialism.

Second, the Russian Revolution and Lenin's leadership of it was internationalist not only in the general and overall sense that has been previously discussed, but also more specifically in the way it inspired and encouraged revolution in backward and colonized countries. The Bolshevik Revolution demonstrated that, particularly with the development of imperialism, proletarian revolution did not have to occur first in the (technologically) developed capitalist countries. Tsarist Russia was an imperialist country, but it was a backward imperialist country, one in which there were widespread survivals of feudalism, particularly in the countryside, where the vast majority of the population lived. Lenin pointed out that Tsarist Russia stood midway between the West and the East; and the Soviet revolution served as a bridge between them. It not only opened up the door to the establishment of socialism in the Soviet Union, but, as Stalin emphasized, it opened broader prospects for the achievement of socialism in the colonial countries.

Lenin had emphasized that a fundamental feature of imperialism was the division between a handful of imperialist countries and the great number of countries colonized, directly or indirectly, by imperialism. Lenin insisted that a socialist revolution in the imperialist countries was a fraud and an impossibility unless it supported, in deed as well as in word, the struggles for the liberation of the colonial peoples, making up the great majority of humanity. He grasped the potential for these struggles not only to achieve independence from imperialism but to advance to socialism, and he grappled with the strategic questions this involved.

The Soviet revolution spread the influence and the beginnings of real organized strength of the communist movement to many parts of the colonial world. Here we need only recall Mao Tsetung's well-known statement that the salvos of the October Revolution brought Marxism-Leninism to China and changed the whole character of the struggle of the Chinese people and the whole face of Chinese society.

And as a concrete organizational expression of all this, the Third International was formed. For the first time, a truly and fully communist international was founded, under the leadership of Lenin and as one of the direct outgrowths of Lenin's line and of its concrete expression in the Soviet Revolution.

Once more the question can be posed—and answered—straightforwardly: is Lenin's development of Marxism and its application to the present era "refuted by reality"? Do current world events, and particularly those in the Soviet Union and Eastern Europe, disprove Leninism—or in fact do they validate it all the more and underscore even more fully the importance of Leninism? It is one of the great ironies of the present situation that, at the very time when in Russia the wolves, swine and vile dogs of the old society, those slaves to heaven reeking of Tsarism, the barracks, the Church and above all of philistinism—to borrow from Marx's description of those who drowned the Paris Commune in blood—at the very time they are pulling down statues of Lenin, the masses of people throughout the world—and yes, in (what was) the Soviet Union as well—need, more than ever, to uphold and be guided by the revolutionary legacy that Lenin has left.

And this brings us to the third milestone of Marxism-Leninism-Maoism, that is, Maoism.

MAO

If Lenin and the October Revolution brought the salvos of Marxism-Leninism to countries like China, opened broader prospects for proletarian-led revolutions in this kind of country and made an initial breakthrough in terms of strategy for such revolutions, all of this was synthesized on a higher level and put into practice in a tremendously powerful way under the leadership of Mao Tsetung in the Chinese Revolution. Mao systematized the theory and strategy of the new-democratic revolution leading to socialism for the countries of what has come to be called the Third World.

The Theory and Strategy of New-Democratic Revolution

Mao showed that in these countries, although there are many survivals of pre-capitalist relations (for example, in China there were widespread survivals of feudalism or semifeudal relations, particularly in the countryside), the revolution that is on the agenda, the revolution that is necessary to resolve the underlying contradictions of society and to liberate the masses of people, is not a bourgeois-democratic revolution leading to the rule of the bourgeoisie and the establishment of capitalism but a *new*-democratic revolution, led by the proletariat, which does away with the domination of imperialism and transforms the social system, eliminating the pre-capitalist economic and social relations, thereby opening the road to socialism. This is a revolution in two stages. The first stage is characterized by the struggle to overthrow imperialism and feudalism and bureaucrat-capitalism connected with imperialism and feudalism. This, in turn, clears the way for the advance, under the leadership of the proletariat, to the socialist stage. In this revolution, particularly in its first stage, it is necessary to build a broad united front of all classes, strata, and groups who can be united to oppose imperialism, feudalism, and bureaucrat-capitalism. At the same time, this united front and the revolutionary struggle overall must be led by the proletariat and its party.

Along with this, Mao developed the basic military strategy for revolution in countries of this type. Because of imperialist domination—and in many cases contention among imperialists for domination—of these countries; and because of the pre-capitalist relations and generally backward character of the productive forces (including the lack of advanced means of communication and transportation, particularly in the rural areas) and the highly uneven and disarticulated development of the economy; there are vast areas in the countryside where the "reach" of the reactionary state is not very powerful. The oppression and impoverished condition of the broad masses, together with the fact that, to a significant degree, the ruling classes are generally marked by serious division and the lack of a powerful social basis within the country, means that the country is generally in a revolutionary situation, though that situation is uneven and goes through ebbs and flows. Also, the backward, more localized character of the productive forces in the countryside has an aspect which can be turned to the advantage of the revolutionary struggle—it makes possible the achievement of relative economic self-sufficiency in various local areas.

As a result of these characteristics—in contrast to the imperialist countries, where the revolutionary path involves a period of political preparation followed by insurrection and civil war when the objective conditions emerge—in these oppressed nations of the Third World, warfare can and must be the main form of revolutionary struggle, from the beginning and throughout. The strategic road to power lies in initiating, under the leadership of the communist party, a revolutionary war: first in the form of small-scale guerrilla warfare in rural areas; gradually expanding the operations of this warfare and building up the armed forces of the revolution; establishing liberated areas in the countryside, which constitute economic, political, and military bases of support for the revolutionary war; and, over a long period of time, seizing more and more of the countryside—surrounding the city from the countryside—while preparing the conditions for eventual insurrections in the cities; and then finally fighting to seize the cities and completely destroy the power of the reactionary state concentrated there.

This is the military strategy of protracted people's war. Together with the political strategy of new-democratic revolution, this represents a tremendously important weapon for the oppressed people of the Third World and thus for the international proletariat as a whole. And while the particular strategy of protracted people's war applies specifically to countries of the Third World, the principles of revolutionary warfare, of people's war, that Mao forged as the underlying basis for this strategy have universal significance for the revolutionary struggle. Of all these principles, the most key is that people, not weapons, are decisive in warfare and that revolutionary war is a war of the masses: this principle, along with other basic principles of people's war flowing from it, can and must be applied in waging revolutionary warfare in all countries, in accordance with the strategic road and the actual conditions. This is another great contribution by Mao to the revolutionary struggle of the international proletariat.

Continuing the Revolution
Under the Dictatorship of the Proletariat

But the greatest of all Mao's contributions is the theory and basic line of continuing the revolution under the dictatorship of the proletariat. This was forged by Mao on the basis of grappling with the new problems that arose as the revolution advanced into the socialist stage in China and by summing up deeply and all-sidedly the historical experience of the dictatorship of the proletariat in the Soviet Union as well as in China. The theory and basic line of continuing the revolution under the dictatorship of the proletariat and combating revisionism and the rise to power of the bourgeoisie in the form of revisionist capitalist-roaders: all this is of great long-term strategic importance *and* of tremendous immediate importance in correctly understanding the process of capitalist restoration in the Soviet Union and in China itself as well as the present day "aftershocks" of these reversals—all of which, in turn, links up with the larger world-historic questions of the world proletarian revolution.

To review Mao's basic analysis: The experience in China and in the Soviet Union showed that, even after the old ruling classes had been overthrown and suppressed under the dictatorship of the proletariat; after ownership of the means of production had been taken out of the hands of the big capitalists and made state property, and small-scale capital and individual ownership had been transformed into social ownership by the state or by collective groups of working people, particularly peasants in the countryside; it was still the case not only that there remained significant inequalities and differences among groups of people in society but that these differences and inequalities continued to find expression as class contradiction and class struggle. More particularly and more significantly, these contradictions—between mental and manual labor, between workers and peasants and the city and the countryside, between men and women, between different nationalities, and so on—were accompanied by the persistence of aspects of bourgeois economic relations (such as commodity exchange and differences in wage levels), and all this contained the basis for social antagonisms and resulted in the fact that the bourgeoisie was constantly regenerated within socialist society. Thus, the contradiction and struggle between the proletariat and the bourgeoisie remained the most decisive contradiction and struggle in socialist society.

Mao summed up, then, that classes and class society will remain throughout the socialist stage and that socialism represents not the end of the revolution and not some stage from which you could gradually and peacefully and smoothly evolve to communism but a transition between capitalism and communism that will be marked and driven forward by class struggle. Further, Mao made the analysis that in socialist society, where the party is the leading political center of the state and the main directing force of the economy, the core of the new bourgeoisie will be concentrated within the party itself, especially at its top levels, among those who abandon the proletarian outlook and the socialist road, who "revise" the revolutionary heart and essence of communism, who take up the standpoint of the bourgeoisie and take the capitalist road—in the name of socialism and communism.

Mao put it very succinctly: the rise to power of these revisionists, these capitalist-roaders, means the rise to power of the bourgeoisie. Not only had this happened in the Soviet Union, after Stalin's death, beginning with the rise to power of Khrushchev & Co. in the mid-1950s, but, Mao made clear, the same thing was happening in China: there were people like Khrushchev in China seeking to carry out the same program. People who had been leaders of the revolution and had now assumed positions of power. But what motivated these people, beyond simply the desire for personal aggrandizement, was the fact that in the face of the remaining contradictions and acute struggles that marked socialist society and the international situation with its ever-present danger of imperialist attack, they sought an easy way out, one that seemed to offer the prospect of developing the country into a powerful modern state in the shortest time with the least risk and disruption, even if this meant capitulating to imperialism, suppressing the revolutionary initiative of the masses, and putting the principles and driving forces of capitalism in command of society.

The answer to these capitalist-roaders, the means for beating back their attempts at capitalist restoration, was the Great Proletarian Cultural Revolution, which erupted in the mid-1960s. This was a living manifesto of the theory and basic line of continuing the revolution under the dictatorship of the proletariat. The Cultural Revolution was in fact the greatest advance so far achieved by the international proletariat. It was an historic event without precedent—a mass revolutionary upsurge of the people carrying forward the revolutionary transformation of society in a situation where the revolution had already been carried out to overthrow the old system and establish the dictatorship of the proletariat and where the economy—in particular the system of ownership—had been basically socialized. Through the Cultural Revolution, for a breathtaking period of ten years, not only was capitalist restoration prevented but new advances were achieved in revolutionizing the relations, institutions, and ideas in society; new shoots of the communist future were brought forth.

To borrow once more Marx's graphic and trenchant phrases, this Cultural Revolution has, of course, been slandered and vilified by all the swine and curs of the old order and the slaves to heaven reeking of the church, the barracks and above all of philistinism, in every country from China to the United States and around the world. And for very good reason: they hate and despise the Great Proletarian Cultural Revolution because it represents everything they stand against, the wave of the future that they are desperately attempting to prevent from crashing upon them. It represents the end of systems of exploitation and oppression. It represents the refusal to accept the reversal of the revolution, the conscious determination of masses of people to carry forward the proletarian revolution until it reaches its final goal of communism. It represents a new breakthrough along the path to that goal. Nothing—not even the reversal of the Cultural Revolution, indeed the reversal of the proletarian revolution as a whole, and the restoration of capitalism that has occurred in China— nothing can wipe away the historic significance of what the Great Proletarian Cultural Revolution achieved and the light it shined, illuminating the path to the future.

China, under Mao's leadership, and especially through the mass upsurge of the Cultural Revolution, was a beacon light and a bastion of support for revolutionary struggle worldwide (this was expressed in everything from government aid, of various kinds, to revolutionary forces around the world, to mass rallies in support of revolutionary struggles, to the story of an old woman on a people's commune in the countryside who told of how, among other things, she tended a pig to do her part to serve the world revolution). At the same time, in a fundamental sense, even beyond the political support and concrete assistance that socialist China gave to the revolutionary struggles of the proletariat and oppressed peoples throughout the world—on the basis of great sacrifice by the masses of Chinese people—even beyond all that, the greatest support was the theory and line developed by Mao Tsetung on crucial questions of the proletarian revolution. This remains an invaluable and enduring contribution to the international proletariat and the international communist movement.

Mao's contributions are in no way negated or diminished by recent events in China or in the Soviet Union—on the contrary, these contributions shine all the more brilliantly in contrast to the bankruptcy of revisionism—their importance stands out now more than ever.

MARXISM-LENINISM-MAOISM: A SYNTHESIS, OMNIPOTENT BECAUSE IT IS TRUE

These great contributions of Mao Tsetung represent an advance of the proletarian ideology and science of revolution to a whole new level. Just as Lenin developed Marxism to a new and higher stage, Marxism-Leninism; Mao, following Lenin, developed it to yet again a new and higher stage, Marxism-Leninism-Maoism. Marxism-Leninism-Maoism is a comprehensive outlook and scientific method that can and must be applied to all spheres of life and reality and in the process further developed. What Mao said of dialectical materialism applies to Marxism-Leninism-Maoism as a whole: it is "universally true because it is impossible for anyone to escape from its domain in his practice" (Mao, "On Practice," *SW*, v. 1, p. 305). And, as I put it in *For a Harvest of Dragons*:

> "Mao Tsetung Thought* represents a qualitative development of Marxism-Leninism. Marxism-Leninism, Mao Tsetung Thought, then, is an integral philosophy and political theory at the same time as it is a living, critical and continuously developing science. It is not the quantitative addition of the ideas of Marx, Lenin and Mao (nor is it the case that every particular idea or policy or tactic adopted or advocated by them has been without error); Marxism-Leninism, Mao Tsetung Thought is a synthesis of the development, and especially the qualitative breakthroughs, that communist theory has achieved since its founding by Marx up to the present time. It is for this reason and in this sense that, as Lenin said about Marxism, it is omnipotent because it is true." (Avakian, *Harvest of Dragons* [HOD], Chicago, RCP Publications, 1983, p. 114)

---

* At the time this book was published, in 1983, our Party used the formulation Marxism-Leninism, Mao Tsetung Thought to refer to the ideology of the international proletariat; since that time, in order to more fully reflect Mao's qualitative contributions to this ideology, and its development thereby to a new stage, we have adopted the formulation Marxism-Leninism-Maoism.

The Current Assault Against Marxism: Distortions and Refutations

But let's get into some of the main arguments made in these times by leaders and spokesmen of the imperialists (and those who tail in their wake) on what they declare to be "the demise (or death) of communism."

First let's start with George Bush's UN speech, delivered in September 1991, and deal with a few of the main points. The following are some quotes from the text of this speech, as printed in the *New York Times* (9/24/91), and some replies to these statements.

Bush: "Communism held history captive for years, and it suspended ancient disputes and it suppressed ethnic rivalries, nationalist aspirations and old prejudices.

"As it has dissolved, suspended hatreds have sprung to life. People who for years had been denied their pasts have begun searching for their own identities, often through peaceful and constructive means, occasionally through factionalism and bloodshed.

"This revival of history ushers in a new era teeming with opportunities and perils. And let's begin by discussing the opportunities. First, history's renewal enables people to pursue their natural instincts for enterprise. Communism froze that progress until its failures became too much for even its defenders to bear."

Reply: First, a general historical comment: As for what it is that the proletarian revolution "interrupted" and "held captive" for a period—a period as yet all-too-brief—it is nothing but the long procession of enslaving tradition, and the binding of the people in tradition's chains. The lumbering along of traditional forces and the force of habit. The history of thousands and thousands of years in which one part of society, a minority, controlled the economic basis of society and therefore had a "lock" on political power and armed force as well as dominating in the realm of ideology and culture. In which the masses of people have been exploited and oppressed, and, through the very workings of the system as well as the conscious actions of the ruling classes, the masses have been maintained in a state of ignorance concerning the basis for their own condition as well as the means for fundamentally overturning it. In which changes—even revolutionary changes—in society resulted only in the replacement of one such system by another.

The fundamental condition of the masses and the fundamental division of society into classes with antagonistically opposed interests remained through all these previous changes in society, and with this remained a situation in which the masses of people (and, for that matter, even the ruling classes themselves) were deluded as to the actual workings of society, and of reality as a whole. Thus we see that, whatever the differences in form—and even in content—between these various systems of exploitation, they all share certain important features and the ruling classes have all insisted on the "untouchability" of certain institutions—such as the church and the state, in one form or another—and have declared sacrosanct the ideas that instill in the masses a sense of "superstitious awe" for these institutions.

You almost get the feeling, the image here, that there was this "interruption of history" that was like a long dark night for all these forces George Bush is speaking for, and now they are saying: "Let's get back to the situation where, without this maddening interference, nations and religious groups are slaughtering each other; where the big world powers are bullying the small countries and oppressed nations and battling each other for world domination; where women are being subjected to subjugation and domination; where the masses, worldwide, are being maintained in conditions of enslavement and destitution—all in the interests of a handful of parasites monopolizing the world's wealth and power —let us get back to that with full force now that we have dispatched this rude intruder calling itself the communist revolution."

Of course, they cannot and do not say all of this openly. In fact, Bush even cries crocodile tears over the resurgent "factionalism and bloodshed" between groups, peoples and nations and the resurgence of "old prejudices." But in reality such things are inseparable from the "history" that Bush, et al., want to "renew": such things have always been and will always be part of the society and world these people uphold, and their society and world could not exist without these things.

It is all this—it is the long procession of these truly historically obsolete relations, institutions, and ideas—that the proletarian revolution has "interrupted" and disrupted. Now that this first wave of proletarian revolutions has been beaten back by the guardians of the old order, they strike a triumphal pose and heave a sigh of relief, proclaiming the death of communism and declaring: "Let us turn our full attention to the business we were engaged in before this 'rude intruder' burst upon the scene."

But, to borrow from Mark Twain, the reports of the death of communism are greatly exaggerated! And the next wave of proletarian revolutions is already gathering. It is already powerfully pounding the rotting structures of the old world in Peru. And it has a driving force in the work of all the genuine communists in the world today—those who uphold Marxism-Leninism-Maoism and apply it in building the revolutionary struggle. But it has an even more fundamental driving force in the very workings of the capitalist-imperialist system—the very "business" that these guardians of the old order carry out in pursuit of their own interests. We have seen throughout history and in the world today what this "business" amounts to—the torment and anguish, the outrage and anger it creates—and we continue to base ourselves on the profound truth that out of all this the system will call forth its own gravediggers.

Along with this a more particular point: Note how Bush uses the word "enterprise"—identifying its more general meaning (an undertaking of one kind or another) with the specific notion of *private* enterprise. This distortion is not only a matter of conscious demagoguery and deliberate deception but also—and more fundamentally—a classical expression of the bourgeois outlook. For the bourgeois, it really is the case that he cannot conceive of effort or initiative other than in the pursuit of private gain and profit.

As for the reply to this, it is only necessary to recall what was said in "End/Beginning" on this question, including the fact that Marx and Engels long ago refuted this in the "Communist Manifesto," pointing out that if this were true—if separating effort from the opportunity to amass wealth really meant that the economy would stagnate—then bourgeois society would have long ago gone to the dogs, because in that society those who work the most get the least and those who work the least get the most: the class in society that is the productive class, the proletariat, is maintained in a situation where it acquires only enough to maintain itself and its ability to slave for capital; while the class that is productive of no wealth itself, the capitalist class (or bourgeoisie), acquires, through the exploitation of the proletariat, more and more wealth in the form of capitalist profit.

On this question, Marx and Engels drew this conclusion: this whole argument by the defenders of capitalism amounts to nothing more than saying that without the ability of the capitalists to exploit the workers there could be no capitalism, and when there is no longer any capitalism there will no longer be people in a position to be exploited as wage-slaves. Or as the "Communist Manifesto" puts it: "The whole of this objection is but another expression of the tautology: that there can no longer be any wage-labor when there is no longer any capital" (Marx and Engels, *Manifesto of the Communist Party*, Peking, FLP, p. 54).

These arguments are related to the question of initiative and individuality. I addressed this question in "End/Beginning," and I will have more to say about it in the course of this book, but first let's deal with some other points raised by George Bush in his UN speech.

The Myth of Free Markets vs. *Real* Socialism

Bush: "...the world has learned that free markets provide levels of prosperity, growth and happiness that centrally planned economies can never offer.... Growth [promoted by capitalism] does more than fill shelves. It permits every person to gain, not at the expense of others, but to the benefit of others. Prosperity encourages people to live as neighbors, not as predators. Economic growth can aid international relations in exactly the same way."

Reply: What world is he describing?!

To begin, before turning to the reality of what capitalism-imperialism "permits" and "encourages," let's take up the actual experience and principles of planning in a socialist economy as opposed to how it's presented here by Bush and generally by upholders of the old order. This is a question that has been widely and wildly distorted both by open imperialist spokespeople and also by many so-called "socialists," especially recently with the so-called "demise of communism."

Here it is worth noting that one of the things these people avoid, like a religious fanatic avoids scientific knowledge, is Mao's whole line on planning. They avoid it for a very good reason: it explodes their cherished bromides and crude distortions about socialist planning. Mao stressed that planning must involve not all centralization, not everything through the central apparatus, but the combination of a strong central apparatus and a strong role for centralized planning on the one hand and, on the other hand, a crucial role for decentralization—for initiative on the regional and local levels and in the basic units of the economy. Beyond that, he stressed the fundamental principle underlying all this—underlying all socialist planning, and in fact all development of the socialist economy: reliance on the masses. A true socialist economy and true socialist planning serving it cannot rely on computers and other "high tech" components of the so-called "information revolution"—they must rely on the masses. Even where such means and instruments of "high technology" are available and can be used, they have to be used, and will always be used, according to one outlook or another, in the service of one kind of social (class) interest or another. The decisive question is, what line guides planning and the use of technology?

As Raymond Lotta has put it:

"Mao was critical of the view of a plan as a technical instrument of control over the economy; plan is an expression of ideology, of the goals and outlook of a class. It is a class-based reflection of social reality that in turn acts on reality, and which, from the standpoint of the working class and its emancipation, seeks to bring about the conscious, social control of production. The formulation of a plan is never merely a question of gathering technical information and anticipating economic developments. It involves class struggle in the ideological realm over the goals and direction of society.... Once planning is treated as an administrative function defined by technical gathering of information and the issuing of detailed orders and the top-down enforcement of their implementation, then the plan begins to dominate the proletariat, rather than the other way around." (Raymond Lotta, "The Theory and Practice of Maoist Planning: In Defense of a Viable and Visionary Socialism," *Revolution*, Spring 1992)

Planning in socialist society, like everything else, must apply the mass line: draw from the experience and ideas of the masses, apply Marxism-Leninism-Maoism to synthesize and raise this to a higher level, and then bring this back to the masses to take up as their own. This is the means for leading and relying on the masses to transform the world through revolutionary practice.

Mao also stressed that long-term planning, even though it is necessary, cannot anticipate everything that's going to happen. Planning cannot be and should not be conceived of as marking out everything from top to bottom, down to the minute details of what each enterprise, or agricultural collective, should do, and so on. Planning should set general guidelines that are broad enough and at the same time specific enough to make sure that the larger interests of the proletariat and the revolutionary transformation of society are being served, but it should leave plenty of room for initiative and for adjustment. Mao stressed that all things, including the development of the socialist economy, advance in waves, and that there is a need to continually sum up experience, to adjust plans. Further, he stressed that no matter how much you plan, there is always going to be within socialist society a certain amount of laissez faire, in other words, a certain amount of people going off on their own initiative to do things—both positive initiative and also some negative things. And this must be allowed for, both in the sense that positive initiative should be encouraged—initiative that represents the attempt to carry out a revolutionary line without waiting for or mechanically adhering to instructions from leading authorities—and allowed for also in the sense that you take into account that laissez faire will exist in various ways and you leave room for adjusting things accordingly.

In this connection, I was recently reading a 1962 talk by Mao dealing with planning, in which he says, in his characteristically provocative way, that planning cannot account for god. Obviously,

Mao had not suddenly become a "born-again" religious believer! —what he meant was that planning cannot take into account natural disasters and all those kinds of things. You have to allow enough leeway to be able to adjust to these things, exactly because they are accidents that can't be anticipated, at least in many cases.

More generally, Mao stressed the need to leave some leeway in planning so that plan targets were ambitious but realistic. To set targets too high dampens the enthusiasm of the masses and can actually encourage people at various levels to violate the plan and undermine overall cooperation and collectivity in order to fulfill the particular, excessive demands placed on them by over-ambitious, unrealistic plan targets.

In that 1962 talk, Mao made another provocative and profound point—that planning cannot take into full account the international class struggle and war. In other words, while you have to keep in mind the needs of the revolution worldwide, as well as possible attacks by imperialists, it is not possible to fully anticipate all developments of this kind within, say, a period of five years of planning. So you have to allow room to meet increasing requirements in terms of assistance to revolutionary struggles or to shift more into defeating an actual imperialist military attack if that comes. All this was Mao's way of stressing, from yet another angle, that you can't have rigid plans that are unchangeable, plans that are so locked into a set way that they can't be adjusted; that in general things will develop in a wave-like fashion; and, more particularly, that accidents of nature and things having to do with the international situation, including war and revolutionary struggle, can all affect—can have a sudden and dramatic effect—on what has been planned. Allowance must be made for this.

So all this is very important to keep in mind in understanding the nature and principles of socialist planning. As noted earlier, Mao stressed that planning is also ideology. Planning is not some abstraction or technical act without any social (class) content. Planning reflects a worldview, it involves the fundamental question: whom and what do you rely on—the masses, mobilized on the basis of a revolutionary line, or highly trained experts in technology, etc., and generally more privileged forces in society whom you attempt to motivate on the basis of narrow, selfish interest, offering them even greater privilege? It involves the question of method—whether your methods reflect reliance on the masses and the application of the mass line or represent the attempt to impose things on the masses, and on reality, in a subjective, bureaucratic way.

All these fundamental questions of outlook and methodology, in other words, of ideology, will be reflected and even concentrated in planning. This is a revolutionary way of regarding planning—it is even radically different from how planning was conceived of in the Soviet Union under Stalin, to say nothing of how it has been approached since capitalism has been restored in the Soviet Union, beginning with the rise to power of Khrushchev & Co. Mao's line is anything but the notion of planning the way it is crudely presented by open apologists of capitalism and also by "socialist" opportunists who, in the wake of the so-called "demise of communism," are scrambling to abandon even any pretense of the need for a planned economy. Today many such people, including not only the leaders of the (former) Soviet Union but also an array of social-democratic types, are concluding that, because in recent years the centrally planned Soviet economy stagnated, staggered, and then plunged into virtual paralysis, this proves centrally planned economies are inherently inefficient and not economically rational and that, if socialism is to be built at all, it must be built on a completely different model, making use of the mechanisms of the market in place of centralized control by the state apparatus.

Once again, as Raymond Lotta observes, "This critique sets up a straw man, the 'all-knowing planner' who is supposed to operate with perfect information and foresight" (Lotta, "The Theory and Practice of Maoist Planning"). And this critique ignores, or covers over, the fact that central planning and the decisive role of the state in the Soviet economy, since the time of Khrushchev, has been in the service of and guided by principles of capitalism and not socialism, and that all this is being evaluated according to capitalist criteria not only by the Bushes of the world, but also by the Gorbachevs, Yeltsins, et al. Here again, an observation by Lotta speaks directly to the claims of people like Bush and the "admission" of various pseudo-socialists that a centrally planned socialist economy is unrealistic and not a rational way to run a modern economy:

> "Actually, there is no aspect of economic development, no form of economic organization, no organization of the labor process that exists outside of specific production and class relations.... Capitalist 'efficiency' is class-bound: it is based on maximizing worker output and minimizing worker resistance, on shackling the producers, not unleashing their collective creative capacities. *Economic 'rationality' has no meaning apart from the class relations it embodies and reproduces and the ends it serves.*" (Ibid., emphasis added)

So that's the first point in response to this particular statement by Bush about the superiority of "free market" economies over centrally planned economies.

Secondly, the practice of present-day capitalism, that is, monopoly capitalism, with regard to planning should also be looked at. Here we see a gross example of hypocrisy—of saying one thing while doing another, to put it simply. The plain fact is that in any capitalist society today, particularly in the so-called "advanced" (highly technologically developed) capitalist countries, there is a tremendous amount of centralized planning.

It goes on at the government level: in terms of central (state) banks, or other government financial institutions and mechanisms, setting interest rates; in terms of all types of goals, criteria, etc., that are set and centralized contractual arrangements that are made for "defense" production and other things that are important to the imperialist state; and in other ways. It also goes on within the highly developed associations of finance capital—large corporations, banks, conglomerates, etc.—both on an international level as well as within particular countries and branches of the economy. Decisions are made on the basis of such planning that affect, at the cost of real suffering, the lives of millions and even billions of people.

So for imperialist chieftains like Bush to talk about how centralized planning has been discredited by the experience of the Soviet Union is highly hypocritical, to say the least. It can be flatly stated that modern-day capitalism—imperialism—could not exist, or last long, without highly centralized planning and a highly developed bureaucratization, which exist in every capitalist economy without exception, certainly including the USA. At the same time, there is a fundamental difference between socialist planning and even the most developed planning under capitalism—whether planning by various units of capital, including the highly centralized and concentrated capital of large corporations, banks, and so on, or planning by the capitalist state itself. Planning under capitalism cannot overcome the anarchy that is inherent in this system:

> "Anarchy of social production is of the essence of capitalism, and only genuine socialism can overcome it. What this anarchy refers to is the fact that economic development under capitalism is not guided and shaped by any prior plan or social purpose.... Capitalist production consists of many different capitals. Each exercises direct control and authority over its respective production processes and seeks to plan its activity and development. But there is no social authority coordinating the social process as a whole." (Ibid., Appendix: "On the Anarchy of Capitalism and the Need for Social Planning")

Let us move on to what is the heart of the matter here. What does "free markets" really mean? And what is the deal with growth and prosperity, as Bush refers to it, under this system, particularly in this era of imperialism? Is it really the case that this goes on so everyone can gain not at the expense of others but to the benefit of others? That prosperity gained in this way is beneficial for all and encourages people to live as neighbors, not as predators?

Perhaps (to paraphrase Lenin) Bush would like to pass a law preventing laughter in public so that his comments cannot be drowned out by the bitter laughter that such statements are bound to provoke all over the world, especially among the masses of people.

"Free markets," to take one aspect, means freedom of trade, without governmental restriction. This can never exist in the most literal, absolute sense, since some governmental regulation of trade under capitalism will always be necessary (which all bourgeois representatives recognize in practice if not always in their pronouncements). But, like every other freedom under capitalism, even this "free trade" is never really free—it is never without inequality, whether we are speaking of trade within a particular country or international trade—it will always involve an aspect of domination and plunder. And all this becomes still more the case when capitalism reaches the imperialist stage.

But to take a more fundamental aspect, "free markets" refers to the "labor market," to the selling and buying of human labor power. As spoken to earlier, Marxism reveals that capitalism is not simply some kind of system of commodity production and exchange where all have the chance to take part equally. This is a system based on the exploitation of the many by the few—based, specifically, on the exploitation of wage-labor by capital. It is a society in which labor power, the ability to work, has become a commodity to be sold and bought, and it is the purchase and use of this labor power that enables some, a minority, to achieve prosperity *at the expense of many others.* Here again is "the dirty little secret of capitalism," and when people like Bush talk about the right to property as a fundamental right, they mean, above all, the right to exploit others. That is the essence of capital, the soul of the bourgeois.*

This essential freedom, or right, of capital is bound up with what Marxism refers to as the "double freedom" of the workers under capitalism. On the one hand, the workers are not bound to a particular exploiter—they are not owned outright as under slavery or tied by the workings of the economic system and by law and custom to a particular lord and master, as in the feudal system—they are "free" to be exploited by the exploiting class, the capitalists, as a whole. This situation is in conformity with the

---

* Even small-scale owners of private property do not operate outside of this general capitalist environment. Individual entrepreneurs, and also artists and entertainers and others who may not directly and personally exploit others, still operate within the context of a system where the wealth that is in circulation is overwhelmingly created through the exploitation of millions (even billions) of working people worldwide. The income and standard of living of such entrepreneurs, entertainers, and so on cannot be separated from this overall system of accumulation and its foundation of exploitation (besides the fact that such entrepreneurs, entertainers, etc., who accumulate significant amounts of money almost invariably invest some of this money in their own businesses—which means employing others to work for them—and/or in stocks, in banks, etc., and in this measure they take part in the exploitation of working people: "making money work for you" means making *other people* work for you—*exploiting them*—that is "the bottom line," as the phrase goes).

character of capitalist production and accumulation and with the interests of the capitalist class: the ability of the capitalist to hire and fire workers according to the demands of capitalist accumulation, without being responsible for the maintenance of the workers' labor power during those times when the capitalist is not employing that labor power—this corresponds to the needs of the capitalists to invest their capital in places and in ways that bring them the greatest return and to compete with other capitalists.

The other freedom of the workers under capitalism is that they are "free" of ownership of the means of production—they do not own land, or factories, machinery, means of transportation and communication, and so forth, which can be employed in the creation of wealth. They are "free" of any means to make a living through their own self-employment as well as being "free" of any ability to employ other people to work for them as the capitalists do. The only thing they possess with which they can create wealth is their labor power, but in order to do this they must sell that labor power to the capitalist, and the wealth that is created through the employment of that labor power belongs not to them, but to the capitalist: what the workers get in return is a wage that is enough to keep them alive and able to continue in this relationship.* In short, the workers are free to be exploited by the capitalist class in pursuit of capitalist profit. And they are "free" to starve (or to eke out a desperate existence in one way or another) when the capitalists cannot exploit them profitably enough—for, as we have seen, an essential ingredient of capitalist accumulation is the existence of a "reserve army" of unemployed workers, whose ranks swell to huge numbers in times of crisis.

---

* This, of course, is not some static and absolute thing. Especially during those times when the demand for labor power is less and generally in circumstances which are favorable for them to do so, the capitalists will drive the wages of at least sections of the workers below the value of their labor power; on the other hand, the bribing of sections of the workers in the imperialist countries results in a situation where, at least for periods of time, the wages of these workers may actually be above the value of their labor power. But none of this changes the fundamental relation between the bourgeoisie and the proletariat and specifically the essential fact that under capitalism the mass of proletarians are reduced to the position where they must sell their labor in order to live and are subordinated to the process of capitalist accumulation.

What results from this is not the fairy tale world that Bush describes, where people are free to benefit not at the expense of others, but to the benefit of others, and where generalized prosperity encourages people to live as neighbors, not as predators. What really occurs is precisely what Marx described—that is, the development of two poles, where at one pole, among a small minority of people, is wealth, power, and the concentration of capital; and at the other pole, misery, agony of toil, poverty, and so on. This applies even within the so-called advanced capitalist, that is imperialist, countries themselves.

Let's look at some examples from recent events and everyday reality in the U.S.: Ask the homeless people in the United States what they think of George Bush's description of the outcome of the operation of the capitalist system. Ask those forced onto unemployment and welfare. Ask the workers at the chicken plants (we could call them the exploding chicken plants) in North Carolina, where on top of and as a result of the inhuman conditions of labor, workers have been trapped—literally locked—inside burning buildings. Ask the workers at worksites all across the country where people are murdered and maimed in their millions generation after generation by the capitalists in the endless pursuit of profit. Ask the immigrants and others slaving in the garment sweatshops and other hell-holes. Ask the workers even in the "core industries" of what is becoming the "rust belt" of the United States, those who perhaps thought they had "job security" but now find their jobs being eliminated under this great system of "free markets." Ask the small farmers and other small producers and traders who are continually threatened with ruin or are actually ruined. Ask the masses of Black people, Latinos, and people of other oppressed nationalities, ask the original peoples of America (the "Indians") about how capitalism does not involve one group of people preying on others! Ask the masses of women who are subjected to the relations of male domination, and everything that goes with this, under this capitalist system. Ask the young who are commanded to kill and die in the unjust wars the imperialists continually send them off to. Ask all these people.

These and countless other examples point to the essence of any system based on bourgeois property relations and capitalist accumulation, even though it is true that in the imperialist countries, and particularly in a major world power like the U.S., the accumulation of wealth, not only from the exploitation of the proletariat at home but beyond that the exploitation of hundreds of millions of people—and the domination of whole nations—in all parts of the world, has made possible the existence of fairly sizable "middle class" sections of the population, some of which are relatively well off economically. We must view this whole question above all on a world scale. Which takes us to the next argument in George Bush's UN speech.

Bush: "Here in this chamber, we hear about North-South problems. But free and open trade, including unfettered access to markets and credit, offers developing countries means of self-sufficiency and economic dignity."

Reply: What Bush is referring to when he speaks of "North-South problems" is the exploitation of the Third World nations by a handful of imperialist countries. International relations under the imperialist system are not merely the extension of capitalist commodity relations on a world scale—which would be bad enough—but the enmeshing of whole nations and their people in the web of *imperialist* accumulation, which, as Lenin pointed out, involves as one of its essential features the fundamental division between a handful of imperialist countries and vast numbers of oppressed nations.

What is the *essential reality* that results from these relations? Mass starvation in the Sudan as well as Ethiopia and many other parts of Africa and elsewhere throughout the Third World—to cite just one horrendous figure, 40,000 children in the Third World die each day from starvation and preventable disease. There is the widespread situation throughout the Third World where peasants are ruined, agriculture is converted to production for export, and the country is reduced to importing food while masses of people are malnourished. And what is the reality of so-called Third World "miracles" like South Korea? The fact is that masses of people are slaving in low-wage industries, exploited not only for the benefit of local exploiters but even more so for the benefit of imperialist masters behind them who control the whole accumulation process in countries like South Korea and integrate it into their larger international exploitation and plunder. The reality is that, while there was a partial and "perverse" recovery in the U.S. during the 1980s, involving astronomical military spending and the deepening of parasitism, from the highest levels of the economic structure, the conditions of hundreds of millions of people in Latin America deteriorated— went from bad to even worse (today, for example, the living standard of the masses in Peru—particularly with regard to nutrition and health—is lower than it was 500 years ago, before the arrival of the Spanish conquistadores).

Countless other examples could be given and statistics cited to drive home the basic point—the basic reality that Bush is attempting to cover over. But perhaps one example says it best. And that is the example that came to light during the recent dispute over whether U.S. military bases would remain in the Philippines: it turned out that one of the groups in the Philippines that was being mobilized in support of the continued presence of these U.S. bases were thousands of women who had been turned into prostitutes by the workings of the imperialist system and its devastating effects on the economy and the social fabric of the Philippines, and who had become dependent on the presence of U.S. armed forces personnel availing themselves of the "services" of these prostitutes! That really says it all—in an appropriately perverse way.

And then we must keep in mind—we must never forget, or forgive—the tremendous human suffering that is brought about through the military actions of various kinds undertaken by the imperialists (and those they back and arm) to enforce these horrendous conditions on the masses and to fight off challenges from rival imperialist gangsters. The recent Persian Gulf war, with its tremendous toll of suffering for the Iraqi people—which is continuing down to today, above all for the children of Iraq—is just the latest grotesque illustration.

All this is the reality when, in defense of this capitalist-imperialist system—and of the interests of U.S. imperialism in particular—George Bush invokes fine-sounding words and phrases about "inalienable rights to freedom and property and person...individual liberty, minority rights, democracy and free markets...." To recall the words of Marx, describing the origins and rise of capitalism, each of these words and phrases from the lips of George Bush comes dripping with blood from every pore. This is the reality and essence of the capitalist-imperialist system whose victory and virtues are being so loudly proclaimed by the likes of George Bush.

The Bourgeoisie on "Human Nature" and Religion: The Marxist Response

Let's turn now to some more "theoretical arguments" made recently by Zbigniew Brzezinski concerning the so-called "death of communism."

Brzezinski: "There was a fundamental misunderstanding inherent in communism or Marxism of the nature of the human being. It underestimated the importance of the connection between creativity and acquisition of goods. The drive against property and trying to deprive people of their own property produced lethargy, passivity."

Again we see here the outlook of the bourgeois, who really cannot conceive of initiative and creativity that is not linked to the pursuit of personal gain and profit—which, in reality, means profit at the expense of others. The bourgeois outlook cannot see beyond a situation where "the acquisition of goods" takes place through the commodity system and in terms of the struggle for individual survival and private accumulation, under conditions where there is not a common abundance but where acquisition of wealth by some, beyond what is necessary for a decent life, goes hand in hand with the inability of the many to acquire even the means for such a decent life.

It is not that communism would deprive people of "their own" property. Communism means the abolition of *bourgeois* property—of wealth accumulated as capital and the conditions of exploitation that are bound up with this. It means the end of production relations in which the things produced are commodities which must be bought and sold, in which labor power itself is a commodity and its use in production is subordinated to the accumulation of private profit. It means the end of the social relations in which people confront each other as owners or non-owners of property. It is the bourgeoisie, it is capitalism, that deprives the masses of the proletariat of all but the barest means of survival and at times even denies proletarians the opportunity of earning these.*

Once again, Marx and Engels long ago refuted these very arguments that Brzezinski is making here, and in concluding the reply to Brzezinski on this particular point it is fitting to cite what they had to say on this in the original "Communist Manifesto," in answering the Brzezinskis of their day:

> "From the moment when labor can no longer be converted into capital, money, or rent, into a social power capable of being monopolized, *i.e.*, from the moment when individual property can no longer be transformed into bourgeois property, into capital, from that moment, you say, individuality vanishes.
>
> "You must, therefore, confess that by 'individual' you mean no other person than the bourgeois, than the middle-class

---

* While, as emphasized here, the aim of the communist revolution is to eliminate all property relations in which people are exploited by other people, and not, as Brzezinski puts it, "to deprive people of their own property," on the other hand it is the case that in the transition to communism—and more fully in communist society itself—many things which in present-day society are owned and disposed of individually (or within the confines of the present nuclear family) will, to varying degrees, become socialized and will be consumed in a socialized context. One example: meals (their preparation as well as their consumption), which today are the province of separate individuals or families and which are a burden particularly on the women of these families. And more generally, with the elimination of commodity production and exchange, things which in present society must first be purchased as commodities in order to be consumed (including not only food but other basic necessities as well as other articles of personal consumption) will be available to people directly, without the mediation of money (or other commodity equivalents), according to people's needs. In that context—in the absence of commodities and money—although there will remain personal possessions of various kinds (in particular items of personal consumption), these will never be more than personal possessions: they will not be a potential source of privately accumulated wealth that can be turned into capital, into a basis for exploiting others.

owner of property.* This person must, indeed, be swept out of the way, and made impossible.

"Communism deprives no man of the power to appropriate the products of society; all that it does is to deprive him of the power to subjugate the labor of others by means of such appropriation." (Marx and Engels, "Communist Manifesto," p. 53)

Brzezinski: "It [Marxism] underestimated the human being's need for something spiritual. Its emphasis on atheism deprived people of some transcendental belief."

First of all, this class of philistine money-grubbers, who reduce everything, including people and even ideas, to "cold cash"—*they* are going to accuse us of lacking "transcendental beliefs"?! Let's get into this.

I spoke to this fairly extensively in "Mao More Than Ever," but this is a question around which there is a great deal of confusion—much of it deliberately created by people like Brzezinski with "an ax to grind" in defense of the old order, and some of it more "spontaneous" confusion—and so it is necessary to continue to come back to this question and answer the various distortions and misunderstandings that arise in relation to it.

First, why does Marxism (Marxism-Leninism-Maoism) insist on atheism? Because there is no god—no supernatural beings and forces of any kind—and to change reality we must confront it as it really is, without illusions or deception. But really the question should be turned around: why does the bourgeoisie (and all exploiting classes) insist on opposing atheism when there is no god? Here it is helpful to recall what Napoleon, speaking about the Christian religion and its notion of Jesus as God assuming human form (the so-called "Incarnation") and all the supposed "mystery" and "glory" of all this, said about this point:

---

* When Marx and Engels used the term "middle class" here what they were referring to is the fact that this class stood "midway" between the masses of laboring people and the aristocracy in the old, feudal society. But, as Marx and Engels make clear, in the "Communist Manifesto" and in many other works, this bourgeois class rose to the position of the ruling class when feudal society was overthrown and replaced by capitalist society. Thus the term "middle class" here does not refer to what today we would mean by "the middle class"—that is, the petty (or small) bourgeoisie (small-scale owners and traders, professionals, and so on)—but to the bourgeoisie itself.

" 'In religion, I do not see the mystery of the Incarnation, but the mystery of the social order.' In fact, Napoleon said he had his doubts about god and religion, *but* he had no doubt at all about the key part religion plays in keeping a system of exploitation in force. Here is how he put it: 'society is impossible without inequality; inequality [is] intolerable without a code of morality; and a code of morality [is] unacceptable without religion.'" (Avakian, "Religion: Who Needs It?...And Who Doesn't," in the *Revolutionary Worker* #538, January 8, 1990)

This is what Brzezinski means when he talks of giving people "some transcendental belief."

But, aside from the intentions and distortions of people like Brzezinski, the question of "spirituality" deserves to be discussed in more depth. In discussing this at some length in "Mao More Than Ever," I focused particularly on the question of "awe and wonder at the unknown"—how this is an important part of human consciousness but how on the other hand this must be separated from the delusions of religion. This was raised specifically in relation to art but also in its broader implications: how human beings having "awe and wonder at the unknown" is one of the things that does characterize human beings and is an important part of human existence. This is owing to the fact that human beings are conscious of reality in the way they are, that they do have the ability to think as they do, that they can accumulate and systematize knowledge, and that, at the same time, there is and always will be a contradiction between what is known and what is not known at any given time—between knowledge and ignorance.

All this ties in with the question of imagination, which is also very important in art specifically as well as in human existence and society more generally. MLM insists that all things are knowable but everything is not and cannot be known at any given time. Therefore the role of imagination is bound to be great, and it is one that should be encouraged and certainly not suppressed.

Again, returning to the question of art, it is one of the characteristics of art that it does not, and should not be required to, adhere strictly to reality. In other words, in movies, plays, paintings, and other kinds of artistic creation, quite often the artist does not present reality as it actually is, but in a different way, precisely in the final analysis in order to get the audience and people more generally to look at the world and at reality in a deeper way.

There is and there should be a tremendous role for the imagination, and neither in art nor in an overall sense should we try to insist—which of course would be impossible—that people's thoughts at all times conform, literally, one-to-one, with reality as it is, or else in fact we would never come to understand reality more deeply and fully nor be able to change it more radically in accordance with the interests of humanity.

All this is very much related to the principle that:

> "We must be able to maintain our firmness of principles but at the same time our flexibility, our materialism and our dialectics, our realism and our romanticism, our solemn sense of purpose and our sense of humor." (Avakian, *HOD*, p. 152)

As I have also pointed out before, communism refuses to join in the deception that there are supernatural beings or forces that control the human condition—it rejects "transcendental belief" of this kind because it is untrue and because it helps to reinforce, not to abolish, the actual material causes of the misery of the masses of people in the real world. But there is nothing more uplifting than communism—nothing which gives greater scope to human imagination and creativity, to the vision of a vastly different world, and to the initiative of the masses in creating such a world through their own efforts.

The fact that the phony communist rulers of the revisionist countries could not inspire people with this ideal—and in fact could not inspire people at all!—is a condemnation of them, but it is more than that: it is yet another reflection of the fact that they themselves had abandoned and betrayed the principles of communism and had become nothing but another group of exploiters and enforcers of the old order. It is yet another condemnation of the capitalist system they had restored, draping it with the shoddiest "communist" camouflage—a camouflage which became increasingly tattered and threadbare and which, finally, they have been forced to cast aside. Let them root in the garbage trough with the rest of the capitalist pigs, grunting all the while about "transcendental belief," but let no one be deceived by the hypocrisy of those who, while denying bread to masses of people worldwide, piously proclaim that man cannot live by bread alone!

Let me conclude on this point by repeating what I have written before in contrasting the lofty, liberating principles of Marxist dialectical materialism with the oppressive "ideals" of the bourgeois worldview and the mean and degrading reality of the capitalist world:

"Religious authorities and in general the defenders of the capitalist 'social order' attack communism as crudely 'materialistic.' They distort the meaning of *Marxist materialism* and pretend that communism leaves no room for 'those spiritual qualities that are at the heart of what makes human beings human.' They preach that 'man cannot live by bread alone.' This from the defenders of a system whose whole basis and driving force is the restless and ruthless drive for more and more material wealth! A system which treats everything, even people and their ability to work, as things to be bought and sold and used to make a profit. A system that promotes the most cut-throat, dog-eat-dog mentality, that justifies anything and everything, even mass murder and the extermination or enslavement of entire peoples, all over the globe, in the pursuit of the almighty dollar (or yen, mark, ruble, and so on).

"Of course Marxist materialism recognizes that people are not mere mechanical machines. It recognizes this in a much deeper way than the defenders of the bourgeois social order and their philosophy ever can, because Marxist materialism bases itself on a true understanding of human beings and their relation to the rest of material reality. It recognizes that, in a way different from other species that we know of, human beings have the capacity for imagination and for all kinds of creative activity. It recognizes that 'bread'—that is, the production and distribution of the basic material needs of people—is the foundation of all human society, but at the same time people cannot live by bread alone: they can and must use their imagination and their creative potential in all different kinds of ways.

"But all this has nothing whatever to do with the inventions and concoctions of religion and belief in a so-called 'spirituality' that is based not on the world (and the universe) as they really are, not on the real conditions of human society nor on the real qualities and abilities of human beings, but on illusions. Illusions which are not simply silly or mere 'innocent superstition' but which act as a powerful reinforcement for systems of exploitation and oppression and as a real hindrance to the revolutionary, world-changing struggle to sweep away all such systems."

* * * * *

"The truly great thing, the most liberating thing about communism is that it shows that we **don't need** anything besides people and their conscious and determined struggle to make a better world. Guided by communist principles and morality, the proletariat is capable of leading human society away from and far beyond the degrading relations and values that are upheld and enforced by capitalism and all other systems based on exploitation and oppression, subjugation, and submission." (See "Religion: Who Needs It?...And Who Doesn't" and "The Morality We Need...And The Morality We *Don't* Need," in the *Revolutionary Worker*, #538, January 8, 1990 and #516, July 31, 1989.)

Once Again on Bourgeois Economics and Bourgeois Mystification

Brzezinski: "Marxism misunderstood the nature of modern economics.... It [Marxism] really was, after all, born in the 19th century, in the early phases of the industrial revolution. It couldn't assimilate the need for complex integration but also for a great deal of decentralization inherent in the post-industrial society of mass communications."

First, bourgeois theory, specifically classical bourgeois political economy, reached its most developed expression before Marxism was brought forth—in fact Marxism, and in particular Marxist political economy, was developed in significant part by subjecting classical bourgeois political economy to critical analysis. So we have to ask the question: which of these is actually outdated?

Brzezinski wants people to believe that the bourgeoisie— which is in reality the historically outmoded class—and its equally outmoded theory is capable of dealing with the great changes that have occurred since the 19th century, while the proletariat and its theory, which represent what is new and arising in the world, are not capable of doing this. As usual, this is the typical inversion of reality by the bourgeoisie and its apologists—turning reality inside-out and upside-down.

In replying to George Bush's speech at the UN, I spoke to the typical distortion of socialist planning and the actual principles of planning on the basis of Marxism-Leninism-Maoism, including the question of centralization and decentralization; and I will have more to say on this later, so I won't get into this further here. But before moving on to the next point, note the use of the phrase "post-industrial society." Here a translation is necessary: what Brzezinski (and others who use this phrase to refer to "modern society") actually are referring to is the heightened parasitism of the imperialist countries at this point and their global network of exploitation in the endless pursuit of more profit. The world today is certainly not and could not be "post-industrial"—and countries like the U.S. certainly do not do without the *products* of industry—so where do these come from?

The fact is that there are still millions of workers in production in the U.S. and in other imperialist countries, and especially the lower-paid strata of these workers are subjected to vicious exploitation, but at the same time there is a continuing tendency for the imperialists to shift productive investment out of the imperialist countries and into Third World nations where they can even more viciously exploit the masses of working people. The "dirty little secret of capitalism" continues to express itself more and more as an internationalized phenomenon. And, along with this, there is the growth of the already huge amounts of nonproductive and parasitic activity and expenditures of imperialist society: luxury goods for the well-to-do; advertising; speculative activity, takeovers, etc.; military spending; and on and on. All this is the ugly, sordid reality that is covered over with deadening "techno-terms" like "post-industrial society."

Who Really Upholds National Liberation, And What Internationalism is Really About

Brzezinski: "It [communism] underestimated the importance of nationalism..."

In responding to this a crucial distinction must be made—between reactionary and progressive nationalism. These are two very different things, and the distinction between them is very important in today's world. There is the nationalism of the oppressed nations, particularly throughout the Third World, which are fighting to liberate themselves from imperialist domination. Then there is nationalism expressing itself today throughout Eastern and Central Europe in the wake of the transformations in the revisionist countries. These are two radically and fundamentally different things. One of them is progressive and revolutionary, the other is reactionary—under the leadership of and in the service of reaction.*

Who is it in this era of history that really upholds the legitimate and revolutionary national liberation struggles, and who opposes them? Earlier, in discussing Mao Tsetung's contributions, his development of Marxism-Leninism to a new stage, I discussed one of the key aspects of this: the whole theory and line of new-democratic revolution, which shows the way for national-democratic revolution in the Third World to be led so that it prepares the ground for and in turn is followed immediately by the socialist revolution.

---

* Obviously, the national question in Eastern and Central Europe is complicated, and while it is true that, as emphasized here, the current expressions of nationalism in these areas are reactionary—under reactionary leadership and in the service of reaction—this should not be taken to mean that all expressions of nationalism there are bound to be reactionary, that there is no question of the right of self-determination involved in any of this, and so on. And the picture is still more complicated with regard to the Soviet Union in particular: there are a vast number of nations, some of which share the basic characteristics of oppressed nations in the Third World, and some of which are rather highly developed, capitalistically; there is the glaring resurgence of the most grotesque reactionary Great Russian chauvinism; there are repeated eruptions of antagonisms among nations that are oppressed under the rule of Soviet (social) imperialism (or Great-Russian imperialism) but whose outrage has so far been directed against other similarly oppressed peoples; and there is the intrigue and maneuvering of many different imperialist powers in relation to all this. A resolution of all this, in the interests of the masses of people of all these nationalities, can only be achieved on the basis of a revolutionary struggle against imperialism and reaction—a revolutionary struggle which can only be carried through if it is led by forces who "discover" *genuine* communism and take up the ideology of Marxism-Leninism-Maoism.

So here we see the relationship in the world today between genuine national liberation struggles and the struggle for socialism and ultimately communism. We see how, in fact, it is the proletariat and its communist leadership that stands for genuine national liberation and links this to the struggle for socialism and ultimately communism, which is the only way the liberation of the nation and ultimately the liberation of the masses of people can be finally won.

This brings us to the second point: internationalism vs. nationalism ideologically. It is only the communist ideology of the proletariat, including its internationalist outlook, that can really lead the national liberation struggles to real liberation—to a real rupture with imperialist domination and beyond that to the achievement of socialism and the continuation of the revolution under socialism toward the goal of communism. It may seem ironic, but nationalist ideology—which, by definition, and despite any claims to the contrary, is bound to be the outlook of "my nation first"—cannot lead to the liberation of nations; it cannot lead to a world where relations of inequality and domination between nations no longer exist. Nationalism, even where it assumes a revolutionary expression politically, in the struggle of an oppressed nation, still remains ideologically within the confines of the bourgeois world outlook, which can see no higher than the boundaries of capitalist commodity production and exchange, with their inner relations of exploitation and oppression.

Brzezinski's upholding of nationalism against communism, against proletarian internationalism, is a reflection of the position of the imperialists. It is a reflection of the fact that one of the fundamental divisions in the world is between a large number of oppressed nations and a handful of imperialist powers; and the nationalism that imperialist spokesmen like Brzezinski uphold is above all the great-power chauvinism of their imperialist nation. In a more general sense, Brzezinski's upholding of nationalism is a reflection of the fact that the imperialist bourgeoisie remains anchored in the national market while at the same time it accumulates, and can only accumulate, on a world scale, through a global system of exploitation and plunder. The bourgeoisie, even under conditions where its existence is completely bound up with these international interconnections, cannot see beyond the horizons of a world divided into nations—and more than that into oppressor and oppressed nations—it is not in its interests to conceptualize or realize not only equality between nations but the final overcoming of national divisions and boundaries and the achievement of a world community of freely associating human beings. Only the international proletariat and its internationalist ideology can do that.

The Dictatorship of the Proletariat: A Million Times More Democratic— For the *Masses*

Brzezinski: "Finally, there was the historical accident of the connection between communism and Russian despotism. The first communist society in 1917 was planted in Russian soil with a strong autocratic tradition, which was then reflected in Leninism and then murderous Stalinism—all of which discredited communism and ultimately led to what I call the 'grand failure.' "

Nice try, but the fact is that the Bolshevik revolution was the *negation* of Russian despotism, of Tsarism, as well as of bourgeois democracy (note how it is the Yeltsins and the Solzhenitsyns who hark back to the days of the Tsar!). Here it is important to recall a point that I made in an earlier talk, "Further Thoughts," about how, to the bourgeois, there is a seeming identity between the dictatorship of the proletariat and absolutism. That is, seen through the vision of the bourgeoisie and the petty-bourgeois democrats who trail in their wake ideologically and politically, the powerful central state apparatus and the blunt exercise of dictatorship by the proletariat in socialist society appear essentially the same as the absolute rule of feudal lords and tyrants, like the Tsars in Russia.

The bourgeois and the petty-bourgeois democrat cannot see— and want to cover up, to the degree that they do see—the qualitative difference between these dictatorships. They fail to understand—or pretend not to understand—that Tsarism and other forms of absolutist rule are exercised in defense of, to impose and maintain, a system of exploitation of the masses of laboring people;

while the dictatorship of the proletariat represents the rise to power of the masses of working people and the means under which they carry forward their struggle to complete emancipation.

To the bourgeois, the one is as bad as the other; or rather, the dictatorship of the proletariat is even worse since it will mean the final elimination of all forms of exploitation, whereas historically the bourgeoisie has often been able to live with various forms of absolutism and monarchism, and so on, and has been able to integrate them into its ruling structures. It certainly cannot live with a genuine dictatorship of the proletariat.

Soviet society, when it was really that—that is, when it was really socialist under the dictatorship of the proletariat—was, as Lenin insisted, "a million times more democratic"—for the masses of people—than any bourgeois society. This was certainly the case in the early years, during the time of Lenin's leadership of the new Soviet Republic. And it was also true during the period of Stalin's leadership as well. Despite the serious, even very serious, errors and actual deviations from Marxism-Leninism in certain respects under Stalin's leadership in the Soviet Union, especially in the period leading up to, during and in the aftermath of World War 2, the following remains true:

> "It is also important to state here that in 'Stalinist Russia' the masses of people experienced far greater freedom and had a far greater understanding of the truth than has ever been the case in any bourgeois-democratic country, without exception. To really grasp the profound truth and significance of this statement, it is necessary to realize not only that all bourgeois-democratic societies rest on a foundation of capitalist exploitation, while in the Soviet Union, until after Stalin's death, relations of exploitation had been overthrown and no longer dominated (though they were not yet completely eliminated). It is also necessary to realize that, however much it may have been marred by mechanical materialist tendencies and pragmatic adulterations, there was a serious attempt under Stalin's leadership to educate people in the scientific standpoint and method of Marxism-Leninism, while in all bourgeois-democratic countries—and this is no exaggeration—from the very earliest age, through the educational system, the mass media and in other ways, *the people are systematically mis-*

informed and lied to about every significant question of current
political and world affairs and of world history and are *systemati-*
cally indoctrinated and imbued with an upside-down worldview and
errant methodology. And this takes place, not through the kind
of extreme, and exotic, measures of the totalitarian state of
Orwell's *1984,* but through the 'normal,' oh-so-democratic
functioning of bourgeois-democratic society and its state."
(Avakian, *Democracy: Can't We Do Better Than That?,* Chicago,
Banner Press, p. 190).

And, returning to Brzezinski's assertions, the fact is that communism was far from "discredited" when the Soviet Union and
China were genuinely socialist. In fact, these countries then en-
joyed tremendous prestige and support—first of all among the
exploited and oppressed masses but also among many in the
middle strata, in countries all over the world (let's recall how at the
height of the Cultural Revolution the "Little Red Book" of quota-
tions from Chairman Mao outsold the Bible!).

What discredited communism, to the extent that this has happened, is in part the defeats handed the international proletariat
by the international bourgeoisie—the reversal of socialism and the
restoration of capitalism—and even more it is the revisionists who
carried out this actual capitalist restoration—in the name of communism. These revisionists have had the worst of both worlds: an
ideology and political line that continues to claim it is aimed at
building socialism and advancing to communism, but that cannot
inspire and lead masses of people to carry out the revolutionary
transformation of society and *does not want* to so inspire and lead
them; a "socialism" (and a notion of "communism") that defines
itself in terms of giving the people a standard of living and access
to consumer goods on the same—or even a higher—level than the
straight-up imperialist societies, but is incapable of making good
on this.

This is what the revisionists in power in the Soviet Union and
in China have faced, and it is small wonder they have become
increasingly discredited among the people.

Looking at the recent events in the Soviet Union in broad
historical terms, it could be said that the Bolshevik revolution
represented bypassing the bourgeois-democratic revolution and

moving directly to socialism.* The rise to power of revisionism, beginning with Khrushchev's rise to power, represented the restoration of capitalism without a bourgeois-democratic revolution and with the retention of certain outer forms, or trappings, of socialism. And what is going on in the Soviet Union today represents the discarding of those trappings of socialism and the taking on of the more traditional forms of bourgeois rule, accompanied by certain trappings of a bourgeois-democratic revolution. In fact, there is no revolution going on—not even a bourgeois-democratic revolution—but there is the more open adoption of classical bourgeois forms.

This is related to the point I have talked about a number of times—how the immediate negation of revisionism in such countries, in terms of the masses (or at least influential sections of them), is the demand not for genuine socialism but for bourgeois democracy. For example, we can see, with regard particularly to the intellectuals in the Soviet Union and China, that what has happened is that, as they have come to see more and more the hypocrisy and self-contradiction involved in the proclamations and rule of these revisionists, many have spontaneously gravitated toward open bourgeois democracy, open bourgeois rule and capitalist economics. This is related to the fact that revisionist rule involves the exploitation and oppression of the masses *in the name of socialism and communism,* but it is also very much related to the self-deception of the petty bourgeoisie. And here a point made by Marx is very relevant: the petty bourgeoisie generally tends to confuse its own, narrow interests with the general interests of society.

I will come back to this question more fully later.

Communism is Not a "Utopian Tyranny," But a Realizable and Liberating Goal

But finally from Brzezinski. In responding to the question of

---

* Certain bourgeois-democratic demands and tasks, such as eliminating feudal relations in agriculture, were fulfilled in the context of the socialist revolution, but that is precisely the point—this was done in the context of the proletarian-socialist revolution and not as part of a *bourgeois-democratic* revolution leading to capitalism.

whether communism does represent a certain kind of worthwhile ideal—working for the common good, etc., he says:

> "It was pushing idealism to an extreme, translating it into an institutionalized, coercive utopia that produced the aberrations we saw in the Soviet Union. In my judgment, the strange linkage between idealism pushed to an extreme and alleged rationality pushed to irrational extremes. The notion that you could build a perfect society according to a blueprint, and in the process you were then justified in eliminating anyone in society who disagreed with you. All of that produced the tragedy, crimes, and ultimately the failure we have seen."

This is a common refrain. In fact, it echoes Hannah Arendt and her "theories" of totalitarianism, which I dissected in *Democracy*. It is also very similar to comments in an article in the *New York Times* where it is said:

> [The Soviet Union] "was the source of tyranny, the epicenter of the utopian ideology in whose name freedoms were crushed and economies were crippled on two continents.... The principal illusion, as Patriarch [!] Alexei had said, was that it was possible to 'fabricate new human material,' to perfect man through the artificial manipulation of social organization. The contrasting strength of democracy and [the] free market, it could be argued, lay in recognizing that for all his failings, man functioned best when left to his own devices." ("Witness to Revolution," *NYT*, August 25, 1991)

First, this is nothing but an undisguised celebration of selfishness. In commenting on this in "End/Beginning," I pointed out that you can tell a great deal about any system and its upholders by what *they* insist on as necessary guiding principles. This insistence on selfishness as a fundamental motive force in human society is a glaring self-exposure on the part of the bourgeoisie, a telling exposure of its outlook and "morality" and of the underlying relations on which they are based.

Second, formulations such as "man left to his own devices" and notions that there is some unchanging—and more than that *unchangeable*—essence of human beings that is innate in them and/or is shaped in them independently of the real world of human beings and their social interaction—these are typical bourgeois obfuscations. Human beings can be said to have a certain identity as a species: there are certain basic things that are common to human beings in general—certain things about their biological makeup, including very importantly the development of their brains. But this common human identity is relative and not absolute, and in fact one of the most significant distinguishing features of human beings in general is their great "plasticity," that is, their ability to adapt and change according to differing circumstances, and in turn to react upon and change those external circumstances—more and more consciously.

Throughout their thousands of years of history, human beings and human society have undergone very great transformations, even though, as emphasized before, this has taken place within certain very definite limits—which themselves are due to the still limited development of social productive forces and the corresponding production and social relations, and not to some unchanging, so-called "human nature." Even what has been considered "human nature" (and what has been considered "rational" and "irrational") has been different in different epochs and in the outlook of different classes (for example, what seems "natural" or "rational" to a slavemaster and a slave is very different; and, as a matter of fact, what seems rational or irrational to a capitalist differs in significant respects from how this is seen by a slavemaster—both are exploiters, but they represent *different* systems of exploitative relations, upheld by correspondingly different values, "morals," etc.).

That certain common features can be identified in human society up to the present time is owing, yes, to the fact that there are certain basic qualities common to human beings in general; but specifically with regard to such things as the desire or willingness to profit at the expense of others; the idea that some people or nations are superior to others, and that men must dominate women; the notion that people's fate is controlled by supernatural forces and powers: all this is the result not of "human nature" but of the fact that up until now the basis has not yet existed for common abundance (note: *common* abundance) and the elimination of the struggle for individual existence and social antagonism.

Before now, the basis has not existed for a society, a world, of freely associating human beings conscious of their relation to the rest of nature and to each other in society. But the point is precisely that the possibility, as well as the practical necessity, for such a world now exists for the first time in human history. With revolutionary sweep, Engels made this clear:

"If...division into classes has a certain historical justification, it has this only for a given period, only under given social conditions. It was based upon the insufficiency of production. It will be swept away by the complete development of modern productive forces. And, in fact, the abolition of classes in society presupposes a degree of historical evolution at which the existence, not simply of this or that particular ruling class, but of any ruling class at all, and, therefore, the existence of class distinction itself has become an obsolete anachronism. It presupposes, therefore, the development of production carried out to a degree at which appropriation of the means of production and of the products, and, with this, of political domination, of the monopoly of culture, and of intellectual leadership by a particular class of society, has become not only superfluous but economically, politically, intellectually, a hindrance to development.

"This point is now reached....The possibility of securing for every member of society, by means of socialized production, an existence not only fully sufficient materially, and becoming day by day more full, but an existence guaranteeing to all the free development and exercise of their physical and mental faculties—this possibility is now for the first time here, but *it is here*.

"With the seizing of the means of production by society, production of commodities is done away with, and, simultaneously, the mastery of the product over the producer. Anarchy in social production is replaced by systematic, definite organization. The struggle for individual existence disappears." (Engels, "Socialism: Utopian and Scientific," in Marx and Engels, *Selected Works (MESW)*, Moscow, Progress Publishers, v. 3, pp. 148-49).

Finally, in response to Brzezinski, Marxism is a scientific world outlook—it is the opposite of utopianism—and Marx fought vigorously throughout his life against various versions of "utopian socialism" that were not grounded in reality—in the underlying basis of human society and its historical development. And the socialist societies that have existed so far could not be considered utopian by any stretch of the imagination—*nor* did their leaders expect them to be utopias or describe them as such. But these societies do represent a great leap beyond capitalism and all previous societies.

Lenin, and even Stalin to some degree, recognized and emphasized the fact that, while it does represent such a great leap, socialist society would be full of contradiction and struggle, to change circumstances and people, as Marx had put it. And, as summarized earlier, Mao Tsetung systematized this understanding and raised it to a higher level in developing the basic line that socialist society is a long transition from capitalism to communism and that all throughout this transition there are classes and class struggle—most decisively the struggle between the proletariat and the bourgeoisie that is continually engendered by the basic contradictions of socialist society itself—and therefore there is the continual danger of capitalist restoration as well as the danger of aggression by imperialism. And Mao insisted that, even when humanity reached the stage of communism, society would still be driven forward by contradiction and struggle—in particular between the old and the new and the correct and the incorrect—although this would no longer be expressed as class contradiction and struggle. In what sense could such a vision possibly be called utopian?!

But we should not leave it at that. In fact, there is an aspect in which Marxism-Leninism-Maoism could be called "utopian" or "visionary." I mean this, of course, not in the sense in which these bourgeois ideologists and apologists mean it—not in the sense that Marxism-Leninism-Maoism promises some "perfect" society without contradiction—as Mao put it, without contradiction and struggle life would come to an end. What I do mean is that Marxism-Leninism-Maoism includes, and must include, an aspect of looking beyond the limitations set by the current stage of human society and envisioning a radically different world in which human beings have been emancipated from the shackles of class-divided society.

The point is this—to take up the terms used by Brzezinski—there is in this vision of communism a certain identity, a synthesis, of the ideal and the rational. That is, the ideal of a world without exploitation and oppression, without class distinctions or even national distinctions, is, at this stage of human history, a rational—a *realizable*—goal. But, in the deeper, fundamental philosophical sense, this is not a matter of idealism, but of materialism—dialectical materialism—it is an expression of the fact that the development of human society, occurring not only through gradual changes but more decisively through revolutionary leaps and radical ruptures, has prepared the ground for the achievement of such a communist society, and more than that urgently demands its realization. As Lenin once said with regard to the revolutionary struggle, it is not only alright, it is necessary to dream—so long as your dreams are in accord with the course of development of reality and if you then work tirelessly to bring your dreams into realization on that basis. And this is precisely how we should approach the question of communism—now more than ever.

This is my reply to the Brzezinskis, the Bushes, and the like on the so-called "demise of communism."

Mechanical "Historical Materialism" and Dialectical Historical Materialism

Next I want to respond, more briefly, to a recent article in *New Left Review*. This is an article which takes the point of view of many so-called "socialists" these days in declaring that the attempt at centralized planning in socialist countries has been, or has ended in, a complete failure. I have already spoken to this general point at some length, but there is one particular point in this article that I want to take up. In a footnote, the author of the article, Robin Blackburn, invokes something written by Engels in *The Peasant War in Germany* to imply that a Marxist analysis would lead to the conclusion that the Bolsheviks were wrong to attempt to carry out a socialist revolution. Here is the relevant passage from that footnote (including the quote from Engels):

"Referring to the situation of Munzer, the leader of the

Peasant War of the early sixteenth century, he [Engels] wrote:
'Not only the movement of his time, but the whole century,
was not ripe for the realization of the ideas for which he had
himself only just begun to grope. The class which he represented [the reference is to the early proletariat—B.A.] not only
was not developed enough and incapable of subduing and
transforming the whole of society, but it was just beginning to
come into existence. The social transformation that he pictured
in his fantasy was so little grounded in the then existing
economic conditions that the latter were a preparation for a
social system diametrically opposed to that of which he
dreamt.' (Frederick Engels, 'The Peasant War in Germany', in
Leonard Krieger, ed., *The German Revolutions*, Chicago, 1967, p.
105.) The Bolsheviks [continues Blackburn] would have known
this passage well, with its conclusion that nevertheless Munzer
was right to act as he did. From the Menshevik position the
important point would be that, whatever his dreams, Munzer
was right to engage in a struggle that could not go beyond the
horizon of some early bourgeois republic. In endorsing
Munzer's struggle, Engels was certainly not recommending an
attempted direct leap to communism regardless of conditions.
He would have agreed with his friend Plekhanov that such an
attempt in an isolated and backward country could only result
in the sort of 'patriarchal despotism' practiced by the Incas...."
("Fin de Siecle: Socialism after the Crash," footnote 7)

Blackburn, rather obviously, identifies with the position of the
Mensheviks, including Plekhanov (and he tries to insinuate Engels
into the Menshevik camp as well!). The Mensheviks, the Kautskys,
Trotskys, and all the rest, down to their modern-day social-
democratic descendants, have consistently opposed the attempt to
carry out the socialist transformation of an economically backward country, such as the Soviet Union and China. The best that
could realistically result from the overthrow of Tsarism in Russia,
according to their logic, would have been some kind of bourgeois
republic, with a social-democratic-led working class movement
playing a significant reformist oppositional role—as indeed was
the case in Germany both before and after the Bolshevik Revolution in Russia. And the worst? Well, as these people see it, it is the
imposition of some kind of totalitarianism based on a bulky, backward economy—something akin to "the sort of 'patriarchal

despotism' practiced by the Incas"! This is how such people—through the distorted eyeglasses of social-democracy—see the experience of the Soviet Union from the time of the October 1917 Revolution on.

In answering this, it is important to emphasize a point that is central to Engels's analysis: at the time of the peasant wars in Germany (the early 1500s) capitalism was in a very primitive stage of development—and in Germany especially so—and the proletariat was in a very undeveloped state as a social class. Although Russia in 1917 was a backward country compared with the other imperialist countries of that time, such as England, France, the USA, and also Germany, still the conditions in Russia then were radically different from those in Germany 400 years earlier! There were, in Russia, advanced productive forces and above all there was a proletariat which, though it constituted a relatively small percentage of the total population, played a significant part in the economic life of the country and was capable of playing an immense role in its political life, as indeed the October Revolution proved. There was, in short, a sufficient material basis not only to overthrow the capitalist system but to go on and build the socialist system and continue on the socialist road toward communism. And, in fact, under the leadership of Lenin, and then Stalin, this was done.

This is one of those old questions that has been spoken to many times, beginning with Lenin's answer to the original Mensheviks, along with Kautsky and the like. But, especially in today's circumstances, this needs to be spoken to once again.

First, let's look at what Lenin's answer was to Kautsky, et al., on this question. Lenin put it this way, during the first few years of the Soviet republic:

> "Infinitely stereotyped, for instance, is the argument they learned by rote during the development of West-European Social-Democracy, namely, that we are not yet ripe for socialism, that, as certain 'learned' gentlemen among them put it, the objective economic premises for socialism do not exist in our country. It does not occur to any of them to ask: but what about a people that found itself in a revolutionary situation such as that created during the first imperialist war? Might it

not, influenced by the hopelessness of its situation, fling itself into a struggle that would offer it at least some chance of securing conditions for the further development of civilisation that were somewhat unusual?....

"If a definite level of culture is required for the building of socialism (although nobody can say just what that definite 'level of culture' is, for it differs in every West-European country), why cannot we begin by first achieving the prerequisites for that definite level of culture in a revolutionary way, and *then*, with the aid of the workers' and peasants' government and the Soviet system, proceed to overtake the other nations?" ("Our Revolution," January 16, 1923, *LCW*, v. 33, pp. 477-79)

Lenin was profoundly correct in this. He was profoundly correct in repudiating this "theory of the productive forces," which pretends there is some absolute standard or level of productive forces that must exist before it is possible to attempt socialist transformation of society; or that, in any case, it is impossible to attempt this transformation in a backward country without highly developed technology such as we see in the so-called advanced capitalist countries.

What Lenin said here was also related to his understanding that it would be very unlikely that socialist revolution would occur in all countries, all at the same time, but was much more likely to occur in one or a few at any given time. Lenin made the following very important point in relationship to this and in refutation of those who insist on some notion of a simultaneous world revolution—or at least a socialist revolution that involves the capture of political power by the working class in a number of advanced capitalist countries, all at the same time. Here is how Lenin put it:

"I know that there are, of course, wiseacres with a high opinion of themselves and even calling themselves socialists, who assert that power should not have been taken until the revolution broke out in all countries. They do not realize that in saying this they are deserting the revolution and going over to the side of the bourgeoisie. To wait until the working classes carry out a revolution on an international scale means that everyone will remain suspended in mid-air. This is senseless."

("Report on Foreign Policy Delivered at a Joint Meeting of the All-Russia Central Executive Committee and the Moscow Soviet," May 14, 1918, *LCW*, v. 27, p. 372)

In other words, Lenin was saying if you have an "Alphonse/ Gaston" approach of "after you, no after you, no after you"—with everyone waiting for everyone else to break through first—then nobody will ever break through and we'll never get beyond where we are. That, as he said, is nonsense, and worse than nonsense. But what is revealed in this struggle between Lenin and the Kautskyite/Menshevik "wiseacres," what is fundamentally at odds in these two different attitudes toward the October Revolution and the prospects of building socialism in the Soviet Republic, is that Lenin had, in a scientific sense, a faith in the masses, in their ability to transform society through their revolutionary struggle. Whereas the Kautskyites, Mensheviks, and so on looked at the masses and saw only a backward mass—they "forgot" the basic principle of Marxism that the working people themselves are the most important and revolutionary productive force—they had faith only in technology developed under capitalist relations.

From the standpoint of Lenin's basic orientation, we can say that Stalin was fundamentally correct in his struggle against Trotsky, Zinoviev, Bukharin and other so-called leaders of the October Revolution over the question of whether they could go on and build socialism in the Soviet Union or whether socialism was impossible in such a backward country without successful socialist revolutions in Europe which could come to the assistance (or "rescue") of the Soviet republic, by providing technology as well as in other ways. This was the monumental struggle over "socialism in one country," which came to a head in the period after Lenin's death (in 1924).*

* In "Conquer the World" I said that, in the struggle over "socialism in one country," to a certain degree Stalin "begged the question" of what is socialism. There I was being deliberately provocative to emphasize the point that the struggle to carry out the socialist transformation of society in any one country must not be separated from—and still less raised above—the overall world revolutionary struggle of the international proletariat, which was a definite (and more and more pronounced) tendency in Stalin. But it remains true that, in terms of the fundamental question that posed itself in the struggle between Stalin on the one hand and people like Trotsky, Zinoviev, and Bukharin and other so-called

Stalin did emphasize, particularly in that period of the mid and late 1920s, that they should support and assist the revolutionary struggle internationally and that the fate of socialism in the Soviet Union was ultimately bound up with the advance of the world revolution—and not just the socialist movement in *Europe*, let it be noted: one of Stalin's real contributions lay in recognizing and building on the fact that the Soviet Union created a bridge to the revolutionary struggles of the peoples of the East, and that the international communist movement must not restrict itself to a Eurocentric view of the world revolutionary process. But, at the same time, Stalin insisted that the socialist transformation of the Soviet Union was possible, and necessary, without "waiting" for "deliverance" from the socialist revolution elsewhere (and particularly in Europe).

Stalin was on the right side in these struggles both in the sense that his line, as opposed to the others, was consistent with and the "logical extension" of Lenin's position and, more fundamentally, because Stalin's (and Lenin's) line corresponded to reality.* Whatever errors Stalin did make in implementing this strategic orientation—and he did make a number of errors, some of them quite serious (even grievous), as we have already summed up— nevertheless on this fundamental point of forging ahead with the building of socialism in the Soviet Union he was correct, and in practice he did lead the masses in the Soviet Union in carrying out socialist transformation and construction.

---

leaders of the October Revolution on the other, Stalin was correct in insisting that in one form or another—from the "left" or openly from the right—the line of those others amounted to arguing that the Bolsheviks should give up on carrying out the socialist transformation of the Soviet Union.

* It is very worthwhile to study Stalin's writings and speeches during the critical years of 1923-29, in particular his lively and substantial polemics. It seems that very few of those who denounce Stalin and distort his role have actually done this.

2.

Once Again on the Historical Experience of the Proletarian Revolution— Once More on Conquering the World

As we have seen, people like the author of this *New Left Review* article (Robin Blackburn) and in general the so-called "democratic socialists" of various stripes, following in the footsteps of Kautsky, Trotsky, the Mensheviks in Russia, and so on, raise questions about the historical possibilities and invoke the specter of necessary material conditions in order to say, of the proletarians in Russia and of all proletarian revolutions: they should not have seized power, they should not have retained power, they should not have attempted the radical transformation of society.

The fact is that the proletarian revolution has not gone the way the original founders of the communist movement (Marx and Engels) foresaw it. What conclusions should be drawn from this, and what course of action should flow from this? With regard to this, as with every other question—and above all every question touching on the nature and direction of society—different classes are bound to have very different outlooks and to draw very different conclusions.

Marx's and Engels's general expectation was that the proletarian revolution would succeed first in one or a number of capitalist countries in which the productive forces (and in particular technological development) were highly developed and the proletariat formed a majority (or at least was the largest single class in society). Instead the proletarian revolution has won victory first—and so far only—in countries which were backward technologically and in which the proletariat was a relatively small minority of the population, existing in a "sea" of small-scale producers and traders (particularly peasants). And these proletarian revolutions and the socialist states they brought into being have existed in a world still dominated economically, politically, and militarily by imperialism.

I have spoken to these conditions and their strategic implications for the proletarian revolution and the final goal of communism in a number of other talks and writings. Here I want to focus on a few key aspects of this and dig into them more deeply and from some different angles in light of present-day world developments.

The Question of Productive Forces

First of all, it is very important to keep in mind that this question of the necessary material conditions—that is, the degree of development of the productive forces and in particular of the proletariat as a class in relation to the rest of the classes in society— must not be seen in some metaphysical way, that is, in absolute and unchanging terms.

Here it is important to stress that, considering the productive forces in the world as a whole, they are in fact very highly developed as compared with what Marx and Engels were familiar with a hundred years ago. Right now there are definitely sufficient productive forces in the world as a whole to establish the necessary material conditions for a communist world, if that were the only question, taken by itself.

The problem is not lack of productive forces in the world as a whole—it is the way in which those productive forces are controlled, distributed, and utilized. It is the prevailing economic and political system. It is the lopsidedness that flows from this, where a handful of people in a handful of countries monopolize owner-

ship and control of the productive forces on the basis of exploitation and plunder in countries all over the globe. It is, as Marx
described it, the accumulation of wealth and power at one pole on
the part of a small minority of exploiters, and at the other pole,
among the great majority, the accumulation of toil and misery and
agony—and today, even more than in Marx's time, this is something that holds true not only within particular countries but
above all on a world scale.

Not only is the lopsidedness in the world likely to persist for a
fairly long time but, bound up with this, for some time the socialist
states that come into being will very probably begin with a level of
technology and labor productivity that will be below that of the
remaining imperialist countries and will not be sufficient to
produce the material abundance that will be required for communism. Further, the development of the necessary material abundance *for communism* cannot be achieved by focusing primary
attention on the development of technology and labor productivity in and of themselves, but by taking the revolutionary transformation of society as the key link and the spur to the unleashing
of the productive forces—above all, the working people—and the
development of socialist production. At the same time, and most
fundamentally, the necessary conditions for communism must be
achieved and can only be achieved on a worldwide basis, through
the advance and eventual final victory of the world proletarian
revolution.*

This problem cannot be overcome quickly for the basic reason
that, at least for a certain historical period, particularly in the early
stages of the world proletarian revolution, the proletarian revolution is very unlikely to occur in the majority of countries—or even
a large number of them—all at once, but is more likely to occur in
one or a few countries at a time. And, as fundamental and important as proletarian internationalism is, it remains true as a general
principle that revolution can only be made by the masses themselves within different countries, in accordance with the conditions in those countries, although in the larger context of the world

---

* I will return to these decisive questions more fully in the discussion of the
principle formulated by Mao: "grasp revolution, promote production."

situation as a whole. The proletariat, where it breaks through, seizes power and establishes its own state, can and must give all possible support to the revolutionary struggle in other countries—in fact it must treat its own state as above all a base area for the world revolution—but with all that, it cannot "substitute for" the revolutionary struggle of the masses in those other countries.

The World Revolution: Advance and Consolidation

This brings us once again to a central question focused on in *Conquer the World*: how can socialist states act as, above all, base areas for the world revolution, and how does this relate to the continuing revolution and the transformation of society within the socialist country itself, as well as to the defense of the socialist country against imperialist aggression?

Let's look once again at the statement made by Mao Tsetung in 1968 about the "final victory" of socialism and what it would require:

"We have won great victory. But the defeated class will still struggle. These people are still around and this class still exists. Therefore, we cannot speak of final victory. Not even for decades. We must not lose our vigilance. According to the Leninist viewpoint, the final victory of a socialist country not only requires the efforts of the proletariat and the broad masses of the people at home, but also involves the victory of the world revolution and the abolition of the system of exploitation of man by man over the whole globe, upon which all mankind will be emancipated. Therefore, it is wrong to speak lightly of the final victory of the revolution in our country; it runs counter to Leninism and does not conform to facts." (Mao, cited in the *9th Party Congress Report* of the Chinese Communist Party, pp. 64-65)

It is very important to uphold the orientation that Mao sets forth here, which is, in its principal aspect and essentially, internationalist. But at the same time it is also necessary, as I have pointed out before, to make a break with certain nationalist and "linear" tendencies still reflected, as a secondary tendency, in this. In other words, to put it in simple terms, the question should not be conceived of in terms of "the final victory of a socialist country," but the final victory of the international proletariat. This is not just a question of nuance—it is not a matter of picking at minor differences of formulation. It has to do with the question of *how* the process of world revolution is conceived: whether the conception is one where each country advances from socialism to communism more or less on its own dynamic, while at the same time socialist countries and revolutionary struggles mutually support and assist each other—which is what I mean by a nationalist and "linear" tendency; or whether, on the other hand, there is a fuller recognition that the fate of the revolutionary struggles and socialist societies in different countries are bound together at all stages and in a concentrated way at certain conjunctures of world contradictions, and that the world arena is the decisive arena and the basic point of departure.

This is very much bound up with the question—or contradiction—of advance and consolidation within the world proletarian revolutionary process. Given that the world proletarian revolution, like everything else, proceeds in waves or, better said, in *spirals* and not in a straight line, at any given time, and especially (though not exclusively) at key conjunctures of world contradictions, there will be the possibility of making qualitative advances—establishing new socialist states, making leaps forward in already existing socialist states, and so on—and then it will not be possible to make further breakthroughs on the same level and to the same extent internationally, for a certain period. It will then be necessary to give more weight to consolidating what's been won, while carrying forward the revolutionary struggle under the given conditions and laying the basis for further leaps, on the international level especially, when that again becomes possible in the future.

As we've discussed before, one of the sharpest expressions of this whole contradictory process is the contradiction between defense of the socialist countries that do exist at any given time, on the one hand, and, on the other hand, the promotion and support of revolutionary struggles worldwide. It is very important to have a correct basic orientation toward this and to correctly apply internationalist principles in this regard. On the surface it might seem as if these two things should not be in contradiction. You could look at it—and it has been looked at this way in the history of the international communist movement to a significant degree—as if everybody is striving for world communism, everybody is making their contributions by making revolution in their own country and supporting revolutionary struggles elsewhere, so everything should be moving together in the same direction and there is no contradiction, or at least this is a contradiction that can be easily handled. But, in fact, this is a very real and complex contradiction, one that at times has become very acute.

It has become very acute precisely at those times when the fate of a socialist country has hung in the balance, owing to the menace of attack by imperialist states, or actual attack by imperialist states. Generally this has been at times of profound crisis, upheaval, and conflict within the imperialist world, all of which heightens the prospects for advancing the revolutionary struggle in different countries and in the world as a whole. Such was the situation involving the Soviet Union in the period immediately leading up to and then during World War 2 and the situation that found China facing the very real threat of nuclear and other military attack from the then social-imperialist Soviet Union at the end of the 1960s and into the 1970s. Confronted with profound and acutely expressed contradictions such as this, we cannot on the one hand say that the world revolution is what counts, as some kind of abstraction, while acting as if the concrete advances made in that world revolution—and in particular the establishment of socialist states—don't really count for anything. This is, in "left" form, a negation of internationalism and a denial of the real tasks of the international proletariat. It is a crucial task of the proletariat internationally, and not just of a socialist state by itself, to defend the socialist states that do exist at any given time and to do everything possible to strengthen the proletariat there in the struggle to carry forward the revolutionary transformation of society.

At the same time—and this has been the greater tendency and the greater problem in the international communist movement—we cannot say that whatever the socialist country does in defense of itself is automatically—by mere virtue of the fact that it is a socialist country—in the interests of the international proletariat. This has to be examined concretely, and the interests of the international proletariat *as a whole* have to be made the guiding principle. The defense of a socialist state, as truly and profoundly important as it is, has to be placed in this context. This, again, is a principle we have stated before, but it is one of those bedrock principles that must be reaffirmed and re-emphasized continually.

It might be asked: what's so important about stressing this principle *now*, since, unfortunately, we don't even have any socialist states? But the point is this: if our orientation is not correct towards major questions that have posed themselves and will again pose themselves very acutely for the international communist movement, then we won't be able to build the revolutionary struggle correctly toward the establishment of socialist states and to continue it, through many spirals, to the final goal of world communism.

As I referred to, all this is heightened at critical junctures—or conjunctures—when the major contradictions in the world are bound together more tightly and things "come to a head." At such times, the contradiction between defense of the socialist country and promotion/support of the world revolution as a whole becomes more, not less, intense and more, not less, difficult to handle. At the same time, the situation holds heightened possibilities for advance. All of this emphasizes the importance of correctly grasping and handling this decisive contradiction.

Proletarian Revolution and Internationalism— The Social Base

Here it is helpful to focus on a point that was raised by Mao in the last few years of his struggle against the capitalist-roaders in China, in the form of a campaign around a classical Chinese novel called *Water Margin*. That novel was used to illustrate crucial features of the capitalist-roaders and key aspects of the struggle then going on between revisionism and communism, between the capitalist road and the socialist road. The point was made in that campaign, using that novel as teaching material, that those in China who were determined to stop the revolution halfway, and thereby create the conditions for capitalist restoration, would also capitulate to imperialism, particularly in the face of a growing threat of outright military attack from the imperialists.*

This relates to what is stressed in "End/Beginning" on the question of "unresolved contradictions under socialism." On the one hand there are tendencies for people whose lot has improved under socialism—and above all for people who, as Mao put it, have become high officials and want to protect their narrow interests as such—to become conservative and to try to smooth over contradictions and suppress struggle, all of which strengthens the forces favoring capitalist restoration. But on the other hand there is "the positive side of unresolved contradictions under socialism—the bringing to the fore of driving forces for revolutionary transformation in the socialist stage—forces on the cutting edge of contradictions that are coming to the fore as decisive questions in terms of whether society will be moved forward or dragged backward.... Fundamentally, all these are forces that are favorable to the continuation of the revolution. By unleashing them and 'jumping in' with them into the swirl of struggle, it will be possible to strengthen the influence and leadership of the proletariat within this mass upheaval and to direct the main thrust of the masses' resistance and defiance against those in authority who are acting like big shots and are seeking to restore a system based on the oppression and exploitation of the masses" (*Revolution*, Fall 1990, p. 21).

Each of these two roads and lines—the socialist road and the communist line on the one side, and the capitalist road and the revisionist line on the other side—has its own social base; and it is important to identify, to rely upon, to fully mobilize the social base for proletarian revolution and proletarian internationalism. And the two are completely bound up together. Those class forces whose interests lie in the thoroughgoing transformation of society, in the continuation of the revolution within the socialist country, are also those who will be staunchest in their opposition to imperialism and in their support of the revolutionary struggles

* For a summary of the aims of this *Water Margin* campaign and the struggle in relation to it, as well as some documents from that struggle, see *And Mao Makes 5*, Chicago, Banner Press, 1978, Introduction, "Mao Tsetung's Last Great Battle," by Raymond Lotta, especially pp. 32-34; and the section "Criticizing Water Margin," pp. 239-256.

throughout the world. It is this social base that must be mobilized and relied on above all—not only in general in carrying out the socialist revolution, but particularly at those critical junctures, or conjunctures, when both the fate of the socialist country *and* the direction of the entire world revolutionary movement are placed acutely on the agenda and can come acutely into contradiction, when an incorrect handling of this contradiction can contribute to serious setbacks for the international proletariat, but a correct handling of it can contribute to truly great leaps forward of world-historic importance.

Grasp Revolution, Promote Production

There is another crucial point that must be discussed in connection with all this, and that is the principle formulated by Mao: "grasp revolution/promote production." Let's dig into key questions involved in this principle.*

Transforming Relations Among People— and Transforming Ownership

Lenin, in giving a basic definition of social classes, explained how

---

* When I was writing "End/Beginning" and "Mao More Than Ever" I also included "A Final Note," with four points which summarize key principles for carrying forward the revolution under the dictatorship of the proletariat and combating revisionism and the rise to power of the bourgeoisie. The principle "grasp revolution/promote production" was not included in that "Final Note," but it should have been. Those four points in that "note" are principles relating particularly to the class struggle—revolution—as such; but obviously "grasp revolution/promote production" has a very close relationship to, and a fundamental bearing on, the question those four points were speaking to.

Among the main things I studied in preparing this section of this book were an important pamphlet by Chang Chun-chiao (Zhang Chunqiao), one of the main revolutionary leaders arrested in the revisionist coup right after Mao's death; a textbook on political economy published in Shanghai in the early 1970s (one edition of this work, entitled *Fundamentals of Political Economy*, edited with an introduction by George C. Wang, has been published by M.E. Sharpe, Inc.); and various articles and other writings from the period of Mao's last great battle against revisionism, personified by Deng Xiaoping. I found these works to be very challenging in dealing with questions that have profound implications for the overall question of the socialist revolution and the advance to communism. I am drawing heavily from these works in the summary that follows on this crucial question of "grasp revolution/promote production."

they are rooted in three interrelated aspects of the relations of production: one, and most importantly, the ownership system; two, the relations of people in the process of social labor; and three, their place in the system of distribution and their share in the distribution of social wealth (see "A Great Beginning," *LCW*, v. 29, p. 421).

Among these three aspects of the relations of production, ownership is the most important. But it must not be seen as the only important factor in the relations of production and must not be viewed statically in relation to the others. This becomes an especially important question in socialist society, where even after socialist ownership has in the main been achieved, there is still the question of significant differences and inequalities left over from capitalist society and their expressions in law, policy, and ideology, which are generally summarized under the term "bourgeois right." Here the whole question of the superstructure and its relation to the economic base also has to be taken up.

In an important article written in 1975, Chang Chun-chiao pointed out:

"It is perfectly correct for people to give full weight to the decisive role of the system of ownership in the relations of production. But it is incorrect to give no weight to whether the issue of ownership has been resolved merely in form or in actual fact, to the reaction upon the system of ownership exerted by the two other aspects of the relations of production— the relations among people and the form of distribution—and to the reaction upon the economic base exerted by the super- structure; these two aspects and the superstructure may play a decisive role under given conditions. Politics is the con- centrated expression of economics. Whether the ideological and political line is correct or incorrect, and which class holds the leadership, decides which class owns those factories in actual fact." (Chang Chun-chiao, "On Exercising All-Round Dictator- ship Over the Bourgeoisie," in *And Mao Makes 5*, pp. 213-14)

Let's look at this more closely. In the Shanghai political econ- omy textbook and also generally in the line put forward under Mao's leadership, great emphasis was given to what was referred to as the "middle link" in the relations of production: the relations among people in the process of production (the Chinese revolutionaries used the term "interpersonal relations" as a shorthand way of referring to this "middle link"). Emphasis was given especially to what was called "the active role of interpersonal relations." Along with this, great importance was attached to the initiating role of the superstructure. What do these concepts mean?

To begin with interpersonal relations: this refers to such things as the relationship between managers and workers in an enterprise, the relationship between manual workers and the technicians and intellectual workers, and so on. The point that was stressed by Mao in his "Critique" of Soviet political economy (and this is also a point focused on in the Shanghai political economy textbook) is that in socialist society the character of the ownership system at any particular stage sets the general framework for the transformations that can be made in the production relations, but within that general framework there are great changes that can be brought about in the middle link of interpersonal relations.

Let's look at some concrete, specific policies. Having managers, and also leading party and state functionaries, take part in productive labor together with the masses; having the masses take part in important spheres of the superstructure such as administrative tasks and the spheres of education and culture; having the masses take part in developing technology: all these break down important aspects of the division of labor handed down from the old society. This division of labor cannot be overcome all at once, but it has to be continually "brought under attack" and transformed to the greatest degree possible at any given time, or else the society *will* go backwards to capitalism.

And, as the statement by Chang Chun-chiao indicates, such changes in relations among people in production (or interpersonal relations), along with changes in the distribution system, can exert a very profound effect on the ownership system. Let's look again at the concrete situation in socialist China. Although in a relatively short period they were able to transform the overwhelming part of ownership in industry into state ownership, in the countryside, where the peasants constituted the great bulk of the people, they were not yet able to make such a transformation. At the time the revisionists usurped power, almost thirty years after the victory of the Chinese revolution, it was still the case that the main form of ownership in the countryside was collective ownership by groups of peasants (and not state ownership). And beyond that, within those collective forms of ownership the basic accounting units, that is, the basic units of production responsible for their own profit and loss, were still relatively small "production teams" of peasants.

In the countryside, within the people's communes, there were three levels of ownership: the team, the brigade, and the commune. And although there were a number of tasks undertaken at the commune level and although the communists in leadership were constantly striving to develop more things on that level, so that there would be a larger collectivity of people in terms of ownership and also in terms of pooling their labor for projects, still the situation could not be quickly changed where there existed not only collective ownership among groups of peasants instead of state ownership but where a considerable part of actual ownership and responsibility for profit and loss was accounted for by relatively small-scale economic units.

But, within this overall situation, tremendously significant transformations could be made, such as having the technicians and experts who were in the countryside take part in productive labor together with the masses of peasants; and on the other hand having the masses take part in planning, in technical innovation, and in administration. Such steps as these are not only important in their own right in preventing the differences among people in the process of production from growing more and more into relations that verge on class exploitation, but they are also important in terms of how they react upon the ownership system.

There was also ongoing and at times very sharp struggle to win the peasants to put the interests of the larger collective above that of their smaller unit of production (and of profit and loss): for example to undertake projects that might not, in the short run, be as financially rewarding for their brigade or team (and the individual peasants themselves), but would strengthen the collective economy and the collective spirit and further unleash the productive forces, thereby serving the *overall* and *long-term* interests of the masses of peasants. And the masses of peasants, and workers, were mobilized to carry out production that was far removed from their immediate and more individual needs—but which served their most fundamental and highest interests in striving for world communism—production geared to supporting revolutionary struggles throughout the world, to serve the world revolution.

To take another decisive aspect of social relations, the struggle to emancipate women from patriarchal oppression; to have men take an equal part in household tasks while moving to socialize many of these tasks; to break the shackles restraining women from fully participating in every sphere of life: all this was not only important in terms of its political and ideological dimensions but also represented a further radical transformation of the relations of people in production and a tremendous liberation of the productive forces, above all the masses of women themselves.

The more these kinds of changes are struggled through, the more the consciousness of people is raised at the same time as the material basis is developed to undertake some changes in the ownership system. (And specifically in the Chinese countryside, such changes would mean having more aspects of production raised to the level of brigade accounting or even commune accounting in accordance with the development of the productive forces and the economy overall.) It's not that the development of the economy—and specifically of technology—is unimportant: this is extremely important, and it is necessary that a certain level of abundance be achieved at each stage before major transformations of the ownership system can be made. For example, looking at socialist China's experience once again, it would have been necessary for there to be a leap in the level of development of the productive forces in the countryside, and in the economy overall, before there could be a radical change to a situation where the commune level accounted for all, or nearly all, of the ownership and profit-and-loss responsibility in the countryside. A still greater level of productive forces would have to be reached before there could be yet another great leap—from collective ownership by peasants to ownership by the whole people (first in the form of state ownership and then, eventually, with the abolition of classes and the state, in the form of direct ownership by the whole of society without the mediation of the state). But the point is that this whole process will proceed through stages, or spirals, and that to remain on the socialist road it is necessary to unleash the conscious initiative of the masses to push forward this whole process through a dialectic of unleashing the productive forces on the basis of transformations in the production relations, utilizing the active role of interpersonal relations.*

In sum, these changes in interpersonal relations, or relations among people in the productive process, have a tremendous bearing, not only on the division of labor itself but also on transformations that can and will be made in the ownership system. And this, in turn, has tremendous bearing on other important leftovers from capitalism, particularly the persistence of commodity relations— between these various collectives of peasants; between the peasant collectives on the one hand and the state sector of the economy, particularly in industry, on the other hand; and even between different enterprises within the state-owned sector.

The persistence of commodity relations means that such things as the law of value—according to which the value of things produced is equivalent to the socially necessary labor-time involved in their production—cannot be overcome and surpassed right away. This law of value bears within it the seeds of capitalism, and it must not be allowed to be in command of

---

* In considering "this whole process," it is of decisive importance to keep in mind that the advance to communism can only be carried out on a world scale, through the revolutionary struggle of the international proletariat; and that all along the way the revolutionary struggle and transformations within a particular socialist country will interpenetrate and interact with the class struggle in other countries and will take place in the larger and ultimately decisive framework of the world situation and changes within it. But this clearly should not be taken to mean, with regard to either a proletariat that has already seized power and rules in a socialist country or the proletarians in other countries who have not yet seized power, that they should have a passive determinist approach. On the contrary, they should actively seize the initiative to the greatest degree possible at every stage to make the greatest advances possible in the immediate arena (the particular country) in which they are struggling, while carrying this forward in such a way as to give maximum support to revolutionary struggles internationally, to serve and propel forward the world proletarian revolution.

production under socialism—it must not be allowed to determine what is produced and how. On the other hand, so long as commodity relations persist, the law of value has to be taken into account in production and exchange. If handled correctly, this can be a useful tool in helping to ensure that the planning and the functioning of the economy is in conformity with the actual objective conditions and objective laws of economic development (such as the fundamental law that things produced represent a certain amount of social labor, which will have to be taken into account even in communist society—although then it will not have to be, and will not be, reflected in the principle of exchange based on equivalent amounts of labor, which is the principle that governs commodity exchange). But the point is to utilize the law of value precisely in the service of advancing from where things actually are toward the goal of communism, proceeding toward this goal in a series of waves or spirals.

Egalitarianism and Common Abundance Under Socialism

In all this the question of abundance is very important. But the question is: abundance for what purpose, of what kind, guided by what line and toward what end? This is related to another very important question with regard to the production relations—the system of distribution and the inequalities involved in this under socialism.

A very important point was made in the Shanghai political economy textbook: yes, it is correct to be against absolute egalitarianism, but it is not correct to be against egalitarianism in general.

To take the one aspect of this—why it is correct to be against absolute egalitarianism—you cannot say everybody must get exactly the same pay, or frankly, many technicians and others who occupy such positions will rebel against you and in various ways undermine the socialist economy. For a certain period, many of these technicians, "experts," and so on will, of necessity, be people who were trained in the old society; and even many who are brought up in the new society will not be willing to accept the same wage as the less skilled workers in production. These technical positions—and intellectual labor generally—do require more formal education, more time involved in the acquisition of the necessary knowledge; and so long as commodity relations persist, the value of this skilled and intellectual labor will be greater than the value of labor which requires less training. Given this, as well as the general material and ideological conditions in society, those who have acquired more advanced skills, formal education and intellectual training will not, in their masses, be motivated purely by communist ideological appeals, and many of them will not contribute enthusiastically, energetically, and creatively to the process of developing the economy under socialism if they are not paid a higher wage than workers whose training and skills are not as highly developed.

Again, this is a leftover from capitalism, but it can't be eliminated right away. So the Shanghai textbook acknowledges firmly that yes it's true, we can't have absolute egalitarianism, we can't pay everybody the same and everybody can't have exactly the same conditions. And the textbook further emphasizes, in the discussion on bourgeois right, that in any case, as long as commodity relations remain, and with them the law of value, even "equality" cannot really be equal, because people who receive the same wage for the same job do not necessarily perform exactly the same quantity and quality of work and, at the same time, some of them have a larger family, more people to support with their wage, and so on; so it's not really equal in the end anyway. All these inequalities reflect the fact that under socialism society still has not moved completely beyond bourgeois relations and bourgeois right reflecting them: to accomplish this is the goal of the proletarian revolution.

And this brings us back to the other aspect, which is put this way in the Shanghai political economy textbook: while we are against absolute egalitarianism, we are *for* a *general* egalitarianism. We are for moving to equalize the standard of living of the people over a fairly long period of time, step by step and mainly by raising the bottom level up. We are not for giving absolute, unrestricted expression to these inequalities and allowing them to grow into class antagonisms and to strengthen the basis for the restoration of capitalism.

In the Shanghai textbook, along with saying we are only against absolute egalitarianism, and not against general egalitarianism, it is said that what we are seeking to create is common abundance. In other words, the aim is to create an abundance that is more and more shared by the masses of people as a whole. This is a radical departure from the kind of situation that has existed since the emergence of class divisions and antagonisms: in all previous class society, a minority, the exploiters, have controlled the means of producing wealth and the wealth produced, including the surplus. And the common abundance aimed for through the socialist transition is specifically in direct opposition to the situation in the world today, where the dominant relations of exploitation and oppression mean that a small minority controls highly developed productive forces and accumulates vast amounts of wealth while the great majority of countries in the world are "underdeveloped" and the great majority of people in the world are maintained in conditions of poverty and torment.

Not only is common abundance important as an overall goal and guideline in terms of advancing through the socialist transition to communism, but at each stage, in each spiral of this process it is important to make further progress in moving toward such common abundance. Understood in this dynamic sense—in terms of movement and not in absolute terms—common abundance and general egalitarianism should characterize socialist society though each of these stages, or spirals. The advance to communism should involve raising the material conditions of the people from one more or less equal plane to another...and then another...while continuing at each stage to narrow the remaining differences among the people to the greatest degree possible. It cannot involve making a principle of remaining inequalities, giving unrestricted scope to bourgeois right and allowing differences among the people to grow into class antagonism in the name of creating an abundance that will be shared equally...some day far off in the distant future. This was, in fact, the line that was advocated by Deng Xiaoping, the line that the capitalist-roaders headed by Deng put into practice with a vengeance once they usurped power through their coup d'etat.

What Does It Mean for the Masses To Be Masters of Society?

Through all this it can be seen how making transformations in the relations among people (interpersonal relations) and also making transformations in the distribution system—that is, restricting the remaining differences and inequalities, restricting the expression of bourgeois right—plays an extremely important role in reacting upon the ownership system in the economy, the overall decisive aspect of the relations of production. Similarly, we can see how the superstructure, particularly ideological and political line and its expression in concrete lines and policies, exerts a tremendous influence on the production relations as a whole.

But the influence and the initiating role of the superstructure is not limited to questions dealing directly with the economy. It is a fact that, in order to carry out transformation of the production relations, it is necessary for the masses to be mobilized to take up all spheres of the superstructure—including culture, education, science, philosophy, politics and affairs of state—for without this there is no way for the masses to grasp the correct line in opposition to the incorrect line and to wage struggle on the basis of the correct line to overcome the resistance of those forces standing against these transformations. But more than that, the transition to communism involves not only the radical transformation of material conditions and social relations; it also involves, together with that, the radical transformation of the world outlook of the people. For this to occur, there must be not only theoretical work and the education of the masses in communist theory but active ideological struggle among the masses and throughout society. Only if the masses transform all spheres of society in accordance with the revolutionary outlook and interests of the proletariat will it be possible for them to retain power and finally bring about the material and ideological conditions for communism, together with the international proletariat as a whole.

Here it is necessary to address a major question: when it is said that under socialism the masses are the masters of society and the owners of the means of production, this is true; but it is true relatively and not absolutely. Given the actual contradictions in socialist society, the mastery and ownership by the masses is expressed not only through the active role of the masses themselves in all spheres of society, but also through the role of representatives of the masses. This is true in the economy and also in the superstructure of politics and ideology.

Even under communism there will still be this kind of contradiction. There will still be the need for representatives in certain aspects. Everyone cannot do everything all the time. But in the socialist stage these contradictions contain the seed of class contradiction and even class antagonism. In socialist society—and this was a very important point made by those following Mao's revolutionary line—power over the means of production as well as over distribution is concentrated as the power of political leadership. And so, too, the power of decision-making in the spheres of art and culture, education, and all other spheres of social life is concentrated as the power of political leadership.

This raises anew the question: what is the role of the masses in all of this—how in this situation do they express their role as masters of the economy and rulers of the political system in socialist society? Here a very important point was made by Mao speaking directly to this in his "Critique" of a Soviet political economy textbook:

> "On page 414 we find a discussion of the rights labor enjoys but no discussion of labor's right to run the state, the various enterprises, education, and culture. Actually, this is labor's greatest right under socialism, the most fundamental right, without which there is no right to work, to an education, to vacation, etc." (Mao, *A Critique of Soviet Economics*, New York, Monthly Review Press, 1977, p. 61)

But how is this to be realized? Here again the question of line and leadership is decisive. As Mao stressed, when leadership is in the hands of genuine Marxists then the masses will have these fundamental rights and powers in actual fact; when leadership is in the hands of revisionists or other representatives of the bourgeoisie, then in actual fact the masses will not have these fundamental rights and powers. And, in turn, whether leadership is genuinely Marxist and really represents the revolutionary interests of the proletariat can only be determined by what line this leadership puts forward and puts into practice. This is what Mao meant when he said that ideological and political line is decisive.

Lines are not mere abstractions—they represent real class interests, both in a general long-term sense and as concretized in specific policies relating to the actual conditions at hand. And, in turn, lines will mobilize certain social bases. Certainly that was true in the last great battle in China where the revolutionary line mobilized masses of proletarians and poorer sections of the peasantry, along with revolutionary intellectuals, whereas the revisionist line was able to rally more privileged sections of the population, together with some more politically backward sections of the masses who were taken in, temporarily, by the lure of stability, the promises of higher income, more consumer goods, and so forth—as soon as the revolutionaries were smashed.

The revisionists insisted that there must be stricter rules and regulations in the enterprises, that the system of responsibility must be strengthened, and that workers must be assigned to and remain at a particular post; that worker participation in management, in technical and scientific innovation as well as in cultural activities and ideological and political struggles took too much time away from the shop floor and undermined "efficiency" in production; and so on. All this was, however, not a matter of "efficiency" but of what the role of the workers in production would be—ultimately, what their relationship to the means of production would be.

An extremely important point in this regard was made in the Shanghai political economy textbook: if the workers do not have the right to question and discuss not only how to carry out production but also what the purpose of the production is, what goals and interests it is to serve, then they are reduced from masters of the production process to mere cogs in the wheels of production—in effect, they become wage-slaves, subordinate to a production process dominated by an elite lording it over them—the capitalist relation between bosses and workers is restored. And, of course, this is exactly what has happened throughout Chinese society since the capitalist-roaders have seized power.

This is why the Maoist line insisted, in direct opposition to the revisionist line, that division of labor in the production process must not be absolute but relative, that in fact it must be broken down to the maximum degree possible at any given point, and that the working people must take part in determining the goals and methods of production, while the managers, technicians, etc., must take part in productive labor. But beyond that, the Maoist line insisted that the masses of working people must take up the cardinal questions in society and the world and pay attention to affairs of state. Only in this way could they remain masters of the production process and rulers of the society as a whole.

Socialist Construction
in the World Context

All this also relates to the points made earlier about the lop-sidedness in the world and the course and character of the world proletarian revolution. In particular it relates to the situation of the socialist states that are brought into being in different countries through this revolutionary struggle, that is, the fact that the proletarian revolution will not succeed in all countries all at the same time but, at least for a certain historical period, is very likely to occur only in one or a few countries at a given time, with the consequence that, for some time, socialist states are very likely to exist in a world where imperialism is still dominant.

"Grasp revolution/promote production" was in part a basis for dealing with the situation that China faced as a socialist country surrounded by powerful imperialist states (and their allies) and itself coming from a legacy of imperialist domination with all its distortion and disarticulation of the country's economy. But beyond that, it was a fundamental orientation for carrying out the socialist transformation of society as part of the worldwide advance to communism, and it represents a universal principle applicable to all socialist countries, regardless of their past history and level of development of productive forces at any given time.

This principle identifies the purpose for which production is carried out—to serve the revolutionary transformation of society and of the world as a whole—and also the means for achieving maximum results in economic construction serving *this* purpose—mobilizing the masses under the guidance of a communist ideological and political line.

Comparisons between socialist China's economy (or any socialist economy) and the "economic performance" of countries under imperialist rule—whether Third World oppressed nations or the imperialist countries themselves—are comparisons *based on the wrong criteria.* As a matter of fact,

> "Revolutionary China's quantitative growth record as measured against that of other countries stood up well. Compared with the growth rate of contemporary advanced industrial countries during the periods between 1870-1900 and 1900-1971, only Japan's performance in growth of per capita income may have been better. Compared with other low-income Third World countries durir.g the 1965-75 period, China's growth rate was quite high." (Lotta, "The Theory and Practice of Maoist Planning")

But of more fundamental importance is the *nature and purpose* of production.

The imperialists and all exploiting classes dominate and organize the production process for radically different purposes than the proletariat, and they bring about radically different results—their "successes" in production and consumption are founded upon and continually accentuate the exploitation and oppression of the masses of people worldwide, the lopsidedness in the world and all the attendant misery. Production under the rule of the proletariat—the development of the socialist economy —must serve exactly the opposite of this: the uprooting of the basis for exploitation and oppression in the socialist society itself, as well as the defense of the socialist country against imperialist attack and support for the world revolutionary struggle toward the common goal of communism.*

---

* Here it is necessary to raise certain criticisms of the last chapter of the Shanghai textbook on political economy where, unfortunately, the textbook, having very well laid out and discussed in very living terms the actual struggle to carry out the

It is important to look at this question of "grasp revolution/ promote production" from yet another angle—in terms of how it found expression in the struggle between the revolutionary forces led by Mao and the revisionists headed by Deng Xiaoping, a struggle which resulted in the temporary defeat of the revolutionaries right after Mao's death, in the rise to power of the revisionists and the restoration of capitalism. As a general background to this, it should be recalled how, in developing the line of "grasp revolution/promote production," Mao made a critical summation of the approach to socialist construction in the Soviet Union under Stalin's leadership.

As I've discussed before, Mao summed up that in the Soviet Union under Stalin's leadership there was an overdependence on

line of the proletariat concerning production under the command and impetus of revolution, then begins to talk about certain "nationalist countries" and loses sight of the very class criteria it has insisted on throughout the textbook. It puts forward suggestions and discusses methods and models for how these "nationalist countries" can develop their economies more independently of imperialism. This leaves out of the equation the fundamental question of which class is ruling in these "nationalist countries" and what is the actual relation of these countries and their ruling classes to imperialism on the one hand and to the masses of people on the other.

In other words, this chapter almost seems to present things as if the various bourgeois forces in power in these so-called "nationalist countries" are capable of acting like the proletariat in power, as if they are capable of carrying out economic development along the same lines as socialist China. So, ironically, the very strengths of this book are forgotten to a significant degree in its last chapter. This is something which underlines, in a negative way in this case, that the question of which class is in command, and whose class interests are being expressed in terms of guiding lines and policies, is decisive in determining what is possible and what in fact will be carried out.

Even if various bourgeois nationalist forces in these countries subjectively wanted to follow the model and suggestions that are put forth in the end of this textbook, in practice they would be unable to. They would be unable to mobilize the masses, unable to carry out the kind of transformations and policies in developing the economy that are called for, exactly because the underlying production relations are not socialist but are imperialist-dominated economic relations and because these class forces are incapable of adopting a viewpoint and line that could mobilize the masses to carry out a revolution in the superstructure and in the economic base to make possible the kind of economic policies suggested here. So in this instance we find a negative example, while throughout the book, taken as a whole, there is a very positive demonstration of the importance of line—the importance of which class different lines represent, what fundamental relations in society these lines reflect, and in what direction they seek to transform those relations.

centralization to the detriment of local initiative; and in particular there was the tendency, especially after initial collectivization was carried out in agriculture, to think that advanced machinery produced by industry concentrated in the cities was the key to building socialism in the countryside and in the country as a whole. Mao pointed out how this was linked to an orientation of giving too much emphasis to heavy industry, to the detriment of smaller-scale industry as well as agriculture; and that, in general, Stalin's approach was way too much top-down, involving a reliance on technology and on technicians and "experts." Mao brought forward and fought for a radically different approach— one that relied on the masses, not on technology and technically trained "experts"; that stressed the importance of initiative from below as well as direction from the top; that gave priority to agriculture and emphasized mechanization in agriculture on the basis of collectivization and in tempo with the revolutionization of production relations in the countryside; that involved a whole series of policies of combining large-scale projects with medium and small-sized ones and advanced technology with less developed technology, giving proper consideration to all available productive forces and above all the most important productive force, the working people themselves. At the same time, and in direct opposition to this, the erroneous tendencies Mao identified in Stalin's economic policies were raised to a principle and integrated into an overall line for capitalist restoration by the revisionists who rose to power in the Soviet Union and by those who followed in their footsteps in China.*

---

* In *Conquer The World* and in a number of other places, I have discussed the fact that a number of the specific policies adopted by Stalin, specifically with regard to economic construction, were similar to policies of the revisionists who have come to power in the Soviet Union and in China. But it must be stressed that there is a qualitative and fundamental difference: Stalin was proceeding without the benefit of previous historical experience in carrying out socialist construction; whereas, particularly after Mao summed up that such policies were incorrect and strengthened the forces of capitalist restoration, the revisionists were *consciously rejecting* this summation and deliberately fostering these very forces of capitalist restoration; and furthermore, these revisionists, having come to power, are applying these policies as part of an overall line which gives the law of value a regulating role and puts profit in command in the economy—fundamental capitalist principles specifically and emphatically rejected by Stalin.

In analyzing Mao's last great battle against revisionism and why, shortly after Mao's death, the revisionists were able to win out, it is essential once more to recall the extremely difficult situation—the very real problems and dangers—confronting China in the period after the upsurge of the Cultural Revolution. Particularly significant—in fact pivotal in this whole situation—was the serious threat of Soviet military attack, including nuclear attack, on China and the policy that was adopted in the face of this by China—the "opening to the West." This question is spoken to in "End/Beginning," and I won't deal with it extensively here. But it is important to keep in mind that the revisionist line and the revisionist forces were operating within this situation, which in many ways created conditions favorable for them, strengthening the basis for them to appeal to significant and influential sections of the population, especially the more privileged strata.

The revisionists put forward a line which had an allure of "having the best (as we have seen, this is really the worst) of both worlds"—making production the key thing, regardless of which methods and relations are in force in carrying out this production; making the acquisition of private wealth a motivating principle and insisting that this is not in contradiction to serving the collective good; and, furthermore, talking as if entering into relations with imperialism that amount to capitulating to imperialism would make it possible both to avoid war and to carry on with socialism—a socialism without the kind of mass upheaval and even, at times, chaos that characterized the Cultural Revolution; without the demand for radical changes in the relations among people and in people's world outlook; without the insistence that inequalities which favored certain strata at the expense of the masses must be restricted so that they could eventually be overcome; without the requirement that privileged strata and leaders receive the criticism and supervision of the masses. All this was captured very well in the simple saying by Deng Xiaoping: "White cat, black cat, what difference does it make, as long as it catches mice?"—what difference does it make what methods are used as long as they bring "results"? Mao very incisively pointed out that this line makes no distinction between Marxism and imperialism and that it serves the bourgeoisie and capitalist restoration. As opposed to "grasp revolution/promote production," this line could be summed up in this formulation: promote capitalist production/suppress proletarian revolution.

As experience since then has shown, ever more dramatically, while the revisionists may have been able to mobilize a social base of more privileged strata, and even certain backward elements among the masses, the line of the revisionists cannot serve the interests of the broad masses of people—or even, as a matter of fact, come through with the extravagant promises made by the revisionists to the more privileged strata.

Deng & Co. jealously eyed Japan and held this up as the thing for China to emulate in its economic performance, but despite all their slavish attempts to follow such models they cannot make good on their ambitions—they cannot succeed in the concrete conditions of today's world in turning China into a "modern" capitalist country, powerful by imperialist standards.*

At the same time, it is important to note how, with regard to China, the situation is different in some important ways from what has gone on with the Soviet Union. For their part, the revisionists in China have not yet at least discarded their "communist" disguise—in fact, in the face of the revolt that was drowned in blood in Tiananmen Square, they have made a show of "reviving" some of their old communist trappings and "credentials." This situation is sharply contradictory. On the one hand, particularly among the intellectuals, the phenomenon of the immediate negation of revisionism being the demand for bourgeois democracy, and not the demand for genuine socialism, has become more pronounced. But there are very clear signs—which even the imperialists and their media have to acknowledge—that particularly among the masses of working people in China (and even among some stu-

---

* Here we see a kind of ironic twist on Mao's denunciation of Deng—that he makes no distinction between Marxism and imperialism! That is, because Deng did not have a Marxist understanding of imperialism (or anything else), he did not understand what would be the actual role of China in the international network of imperialist relations once he seized power and set about restoring capitalism: because his method was not that of Marxist materialism, he could not recognize the impossibility, under present world conditions, of realizing his "ideal" of turning China into a major world (imperialist) power.

dents and intellectuals) there are those who recognize a radical difference between the phony "communism" of Deng and Co. and the real, revolutionary communism of Mao and his comrades, and who can once again be won to the understanding that, to paraphrase Mao himself, "only Maoism can save China"—and, in the same spirit, only Maoism can save the world—only Marxism-Leninism-Maoism points the way to real emancipation for the masses of people in China and worldwide.

CONCLUSION:

THE IDEOLOGICAL CONFRONTATION

First of all, I want to discuss this in more immediate terms—the ideological offensive of the imperialists and our ideological counteroffensive:

The recent events in the Soviet Union, on top of the other major developments in the revisionist countries in the past few years, have heightened the importance of the ideological struggle. As has been pointed out, through their stepped-up ideological offensive against communism the imperialists have made communism a broad mass question, and although the terms in which this is being posed by the enemy, and "spontaneously" among the people, are not themselves favorable, there is a very favorable aspect in this which must be seized on. To repeat once again an important point of orientation: even though, in the final analysis and overall, the response to the imperialists and their ideological offensive must be delivered in the material sphere—and particularly in the political struggle, taking its highest form of people's war when the conditions for that exist or emerge—still we must not underestimate the importance of the ideological struggle or the opportunities for waging that struggle in the current situation especially.

We must not only answer their distortions around the current events and bring to light the actual underlying motive forces and class interests, but we must speak to the larger questions bound up with this—involving not only matters of economics and politics but also fundamental ideological questions, such as "human nature" and the possibility of radically changing human society and the people who make it up. We must bring forward our world outlook, apply it in a living way, and popularize its basic principles. This is where the immediate ideological battle links up with the more general and fundamental struggle between the two basically opposed world outlooks—the proletarian and the bourgeois.

Two World Outlooks— Two Opposing Views of Freedom

In the world today, there are only two classes capable of running society: the bourgeoisie and the proletariat. The present era of world history is marked by the struggle between these two antagonistically opposed classes, and this era will only be superseded when that struggle is resolved through the triumph of the proletariat and the advance from the epoch of capitalism to the epoch of communism worldwide. This is a struggle without precedent in human history. This is so because the proletarian revolution represents a leap beyond the situation where people's material conditions and corresponding social relations and ideas have made it impossible for them to enter into voluntary association on the basis of a conscious grasp of the real motive forces and fundamental relations in nature, in society, and in the thinking of people. This revolution represents, as Marx and Engels put it in the "Communist Manifesto," the radical rupture with traditional property relations and with traditional ideas. And the bourgeoisie stands as the last barrier to making that leap, the last shackle holding back those radical ruptures.

For all these reasons, the struggle between these two forces is bound to be a monumental one, battled out in every sphere. And the ideological struggle is a crucial field of battle, exerting a great influence on the overall conflict. On every decisive question, from the nature of human beings to the nature and content of freedom, bourgeois and proletarian ideology are fundamentally in opposition. These ideologies reflect radically different worlds: one passing, amidst massive convulsion, into extinction; the other experiencing the painful pangs of birth.

The bourgeois declares his system and values eternal—but that is merely a tautology—because he cannot see beyond the boundaries of bourgeois society. The bourgeoisie cannot recognize or acknowledge that its hallowed ideals have already become hollow because they are the expression of material conditions and social relations which have become historically, if not yet actually, obsolete. Let us examine how this is so.

First of all, there is the whole domination of commodity relations that characterizes bourgeois society, and with it what Marx described as "commodity fetishism" and, along with that, bourgeois individualism. These are all made guiding and sacred principles by the guardians of the old order, by the upholders and defenders of capitalism and imperialism.

What Marx meant by "commodity fetishism" in particular is that the underlying relationships among people that are at the foundation of society—the whole basic reality that is revealed by historical materialism, the fact that social labor carried out by people entering into definite relations of production is the foundation of society and of its institutions and ideas—this is *disguised* in commodity-producing society. People confront each other through the commodities they own. *Things* are in relationship to each other—money is being exchanged for a particular thing, which in turn is being exchanged for money, and so on and so forth—it appears that this is the essence of what goes on in society. In these relations, people appear to be just so many individuals who just happen to have this or that commodity—their possession of particular commodities appears to be accidental or at any rate the product of their own individual effort or enterprise. The fact that they are part of a larger social division of labor and that the particular way in which they earn their livelihood (or accumulate wealth) is ultimately determined by that social division of labor and by the process of production and exchange in society, and ultimately the world, as a whole...this is obscured, concealed.

Along with this goes bourgeois individualism, the notion that each person has to look out for her or himself first and above all and in opposition to everyone else. This outlook of "look out for No. 1" is in accord with commodity relations, where people are involved not simply in exchange with others through the medium of their commodities, but also in competition with each other, a competition in which some prosper and others lose out (this is an expression of commodity production's inherent anarchy, which stems from the fact that commodities are things produced not for immediate use but for exchange, but no one can be certain how much demand there will be for a particular commodity). The relation of individuals as equal commodity owners—equal at least in the sense that they all share the common status of being commodity owners in a society where commodity value is the uniform measure of exchange relations—this is still only the outward appearance. And this is even the outward appearance of the relation between the workers and the capitalists. But, in fact, this is camouflage over the actual inner essence of capitalism and its process of accumulation—the relation of exploitation and oppression of the working class by the capitalist class.

Correspondingly, the bourgeois notion of "freedom" involves the *appearance* of individuality—the appearance that the individual is sovereign, that the individual and her or his rights are the highest priority and the object of politics and law. The *essence* is that individuality is subsumed in class relations—class relations of exploitation and oppression. And even in its outward appearance, bourgeois individuality and the corresponding notions of freedom are cast in negative terms: in terms of the rights of one not impinging on the rights of others; in terms of the rights of individuals being protected against infringement by other individuals, as well as by the state.

This view of freedom, while on the one hand it involves an aspect of illusion—in the way in which it conceals the more fundamental relations and inner essence of capitalist exploitation—at the same time does reveal something of that inner essence, of the social antagonism bound up with capital. This is related to the fact that, although commodity relations in and of themselves do not necessarily involve social antagonism and class exploitation, nevertheless they contain the seeds of this antagonism and exploitation.*

As we have seen, commodity relations are not simply relations of equality (based on the principle of exchange of equal values) but also contain an aspect of competition and rivalry. Thus, even the notions of individuality and freedom that correspond to commodity relations in their outer appearance and general form, and not specifically to relations between the bourgeoisie and the proletariat, still find expression in terms of the clash of individual interests and "wills." In this respect, there is a real identity between such notions and the actual nature of capitalist society. Further, commodity relations contain the germ, or hold the potential, of relations in which labor power itself has become a commodity. And, to a certain degree at least, there is a conscious recognition of this fact in bourgeois society generally, particularly in the understanding that in order to get rich it is necessary to go beyond being a mere owner of commodities, beyond even a self-employed owner of means of production, and become an employer (and in that capacity an owner and user) of the labor power of others—in short, to become a capitalist exploiter. Here is the deeper meaning of the expression: capitalism is a dog-eat-dog society and it has a dog-eat-dog philosophy.

Bourgeois society and its rulers, through their media, their educational system and culture, and in other ways, focus attention on the few who are wealthy and privileged: this is what is held up for the masses to emulate or to worship from their lowly position. The fact that this wealth and privilege are directly related to, are at the expense of, the many who are poor and oppressed throughout the world—the fact that the domination of bourgeois private property in the world means conditions of privation for the world's great majority—this profound fact is covered over. The

* Mao, in "On Contradiction," quoted Lenin, from "On the Question of Dialectics," on how in the exchange of commodities "analysis reveals *all* the contradictions (or the germs of *all* the contradictions) of modern [bourgeois] society." (See Mao, *SW*, v. 1. p. 319.)

present production and social relations in the world are declared to be eternal and the prevailing system is proclaimed the best of all possible systems. The "loftiest" goal that is promoted is to rise within the corrupting confines of the system, in ruthless competition with others.

The class-conscious proletariat and its outlook and culture focus on the masses of people, worldwide—on their conditions of subjugation and suffering, but more than that, and above all, on their revolutionary struggles and their potential to turn the bourgeois world upside-down (or rightside-up), to completely transform the world and the condition of humanity as a whole. On this basis, the appeal is made to the broadest ranks of the people to unite with the political program of the revolutionary proletariat but also to take up its viewpoint and vision and remold their world outlook, rupturing with the whole mentality of surviving (or prospering) through cut-throat competition and profiting at the expense of others. The truly lofty goal that is held up is not to "rise within" the prevailing system but to rise up and overthrow this system and put an end to all systems, and all relations, in which the fortune of the few means the misery of the many: to replace this with a human society in which people realize their interests in common, in which cooperation will be as "natural" as competition seems to be now.

Thus, the proletarian-communist vision of freedom is radically and profoundly different from the bourgeois. The communist vision of freedom involves fundamentally and essentially the abolition of conditions of enslavement of any kind—the abolition of all exploitation and oppression and, indeed, the abolition of all class distinctions and social antagonisms. It envisions, yes, the freeing of individuals from these relations of exploitation and oppression, but it does not envision a situation where each individual independently pursues her or his own individual interests divorced from or over and against society. Communism continues to recognize that individuals must and will come together in society in order to realize their collective interests (and their interests as individuals). And that it is only *in and through* society— and fundamentally in and through the process of producing and reproducing the material requirements of life—that people can realize an increasing dimension of freedom. This fundamental principle will continue to apply in communist society, though it will apply there in a radically different way than in any previous human society.

In communist society there will be freedom for individuals on a whole new level, and there will be a broadened scope for individuality, but there will *not* be *individualism*—that is, it will not be a significant social problem. People will not be bound within the limits of the individual struggle for existence, nor motivated by the drive to acquire wealth at the expense of others. People will consciously, voluntarily subordinate themselves to the higher interests of society as a whole. They will grasp their true relations with each other in society and with nature, through society. They will act in accordance with the understanding that people's freedom to engage themselves in spheres other than work, as well as the nature of work itself—whether it is alienating or fulfilling, a negation of people's will or an expression of it—depends on the character of the social, and above all production, relations and the overall development of the productive forces. They will be conscious of the fact that the basis exists, and with it the necessity, to continually elevate the material, social, and cultural conditions of the members of society *in common*. They will grasp that everyone's interests are realized through the transformation of society, to expand the sphere of freedom for all. This is the profound point that Marx made in his succinct statement that "Right can never be higher than the economic structure of society and its cultural development conditioned thereby" (Marx, *Critique of the Gotha Programme*, Peking, FLP, p. 17).

Mao spoke to this question in giving a concise description of communism: "The epoch of world communism will be reached when all mankind voluntarily and consciously changes itself and the world" (Mao, "On Practice," *SW*, v. 1, p. 308). The meaning and implications of this are discussed at some length in the final chapter of *Democracy: Can't We Do Better Than That?* There it is pointed out that communism understands the essence of freedom as the recognition and transformation of necessity; that this process—

involving the dialectical relation (contradiction) between necessity and freedom—is a never-ending one, though it finds different expression in different circumstances; and that in communist society this will find a qualitatively new and different expression, because there will not be the obstructing and obscuring effects of class division, social antagonism, and the lack of common abundance. The following passage from that chapter gives a basic sense of what is said there concerning the essential character of communist society and its guiding principles:

> "There will still be contradictions among the people, and indeed the struggle to resolve these will be a driving force in society, but there will not be contradictions between the people and the enemy...there will not be people who are enemies. There will still be compulsion, in the sense of necessity, but there will *not be social compulsion in the sense of the political domination of one part of society over another or the domination of one individual over another.* In the absence of such antagonism and compulsion, people will voluntarily unite—and struggle, often sharply no doubt, but nonantagonistically—to continually confront and transform necessity....
>
> "The abolition of social antagonism and political domination, and the unity of people around the basic principles of dialectical materialism—together with the struggle over how to apply and further develop them—will make possible, for the first time, the voluntary association of people in society on the basis of a fundamentally correct and ever-deepening understanding of the laws of motion of nature, of society, and of the relation between the two—it will make possible and involve the recognition and transformation of necessity on a whole new and far higher basis than humanity has previously been capable of." (Avakian, *Democracy*, pp. 265-66)

Moving Beyond Bourgeois Right

In the light of what has been said so far, I want to specifically focus on a basic principle of communism: "from each according to his ability, to each according to his needs." In particular, I want to speak to what this principle actually means, and why it is realizable. First, let's look at the following basic summary from Marx on the necessary conditions for the realization of this principle:

"...after the enslaving subordination of the individual to the division of labor, and with it also the antithesis between mental and physical labor, has vanished; after labor has become not only a means of life but itself life's prime want; after the productive forces have also increased with the all-round development of the individual, and all the springs of co-operative wealth flow more abundantly—only then can the narrow horizon of bourgeois right be crossed in its entirety and society inscribe on its banners: From each according to his ability, to each according to his needs!" (Marx, *Critique of the Gotha Programme*, p. 17)

How are we to understand the fuller implications of this? This principle—"From each according to his ability, to each according to his needs"—is not simply a principle of distribution or a principle describing only the relationship between production and distribution in communist society. It does describe this, but at the same time it reflects, in a concentrated way, definite material conditions, social relations, and ideas. In order for this principle to be realizable, the necessary *material conditions* have to be achieved— that is, there has to be a situation where the development of the productive forces and the production of a common abundance has proceeded together with the transformation of the production and social relations such that the division between mental and manual labor, and oppressive division of labor generally, can be overcome and the needs of society and of individuals can be met on a continually advancing level. Together with this, there has to be the abolition of commodity relations, including their generalized expression in the form of money, which will have to be replaced by a medium of exchange that does not reflect commodity relations and does not contain the seed of capitalist (or other) exploitation.*

But the necessary *ideological conditions* must also have been

---

* As discussed earlier, the achievement of these conditions must take place on a world scale, through a long and tortuous process of revolutionary transformation in which there will be uneven development, the seizure of power in different countries at different times, and a complex dialectical interplay between the revolutionary struggles and the revolutionization of society in these different countries—a dialectic in which the world arena is fundamentally and ultimately decisive while the mutually interacting and mutually supporting struggles of the proletarians in different countries constitute the key link in fundamentally transforming the world as a whole.

achieved—there must be a generalized communist consciousness in society. In other words, if "ability" and "needs" are still conceived of in terms of the bourgeois conception of freedom and in terms of individualism, there is no way this principle can work: people will not contribute to society according to their abilities, nor will they be able to correctly work out how to receive back from society according to their needs. The whole notion of communism—and the whole notion of the first part of this slogan "from each according to his ability..."—means that people no longer are required to, and no longer do, work in order to meet their own individual and immediate needs. Society will have advanced to the point where there is a common abundance and the means for continually increasing that abundance, so that people's basic individual existence is no longer a question: it will be assured to the point where it no longer has to be a focus of attention. People will not work with that requirement or necessity in mind, but in order to contribute to society all they can according to their abilities.

At the same time, they will receive back from society according to their needs, not as such needs would be conceived of from the point of view of bourgeois society—not in order to acquire more than others and to strive to turn accumulated wealth into the ability to exploit others—but in accordance with the principle of raising the material conditions and expanding the sphere of freedom of the people in society as a whole and in common, as discussed earlier. Here it is important to keep in mind that needs are not absolute or abstract but are concrete and are socially determined—they flow from what society is capable of producing at any given stage and what the prevailing relations and ideas are in that society. This applies to communist society as well.*

In communist society, needs will be determined in terms of what will enable everyone in society to continue developing in an

---

* Human beings do have certain basic needs for survival, but the ways in which people attempt to meet these needs, the specific objects they consume, how these are acquired, etc., are all socially determined; beyond that, and more generally, the needs of people are determined by the character of the productive forces and production relations—and the corresponding superstructure—in the given society.

all-around way, intellectually as well as physically; and what will at the same time enable society to continue raising the level of common abundance and continue transforming social relations so that the *level* from which the all-around development of the people is carried forward can be continually *elevated* in an *upward spiral.*

Technology—and Ideology

The bourgeoisie and its ideologists say all of this is impossible on both technological and ideological grounds. They insist that today's modern technology does not allow for the type of centralism that communism involves, and that, in any case, production cannot be subjected to the kind of conscious control that communism envisions. At the same time, they insist that people are not capable of acting consciously in the higher interests of humanity and can only be motivated by acquisitiveness and self-aggrandizement as the "bottom line." They are wrong on both grounds.

Communist society will utilize advanced technology, and will continue to develop it. But this will not be equated with more and more centralization, and technology will not be developed in a way that results in the domination of technology over the people—that is a hallmark of capitalism. Nor will this be equated with short-sighted use of technology, at the expense of the larger interests of humanity and of future generations—that, too, is a hallmark of capitalism. Communism and the common abundance that characterizes it will not mean an extension of the same kind of social organization that now dominates, and distorts, the world— it will not be simply a higher level of output based on the same relations and values. It will not be some kind of "more equitable" distribution of "imperialist plenty." It will involve a difference not just in quantity of output, taking the world as a whole, but more than that a radical difference *qualitatively*—in the whole way the question of production and its connection to social relations and values is approached.

Questions of ecology which are being broadly taken up in society today are very much involved here. It is very important to recall and to call to people's attention the great strides that were made in this sphere in socialist China, even in a society still divided into classes and a world still dominated by imperialism. They were able to make tremendous strides in converting so-called waste into useful products and in taking into account ecological questions and the interests of future generations. They were able to do this because they were not driven by the anarchy of capitalism and the never-ending pursuit of greater capitalist profit without regard to the effect on the environment, on the ecological system.

When humanity reaches communism, the people, guided by communist ideology, will command technology. That will open possibilities for all kinds of things impossible and largely even unimaginable under any previous society, in terms of meeting the all-around needs of the people and society, not only at the time but with future generations in mind. Here it is worthwhile recalling Marx's comment in *Capital* that:

> "From the standpoint of a higher economic form of society, private ownership of the globe by single individuals will appear quite as absurd as private ownership of one man by another. Even a whole society, a nation, or even all simultaneously existing societies taken together, are not the owners of the globe. They are only its possessors, its usufructuaries, and, like *boni patres familias*, they must hand it down to succeeding generations in an improved condition." (Marx, *Capital*, v. 3, Introductory Section of Chapter 46, p. 776)

Communism will be a great leap forward for humanity, beyond horizons that can only be dimly glimpsed today. Like reality in general, communist society will be marked by contradiction and struggle—it will be driven forward by contradiction and struggle—but this will not be such that the basic interests of individuals or of groups will be in fundamental conflict with each other. Class divisions, all class distinctions, will have been eliminated. But also such things as the struggle for mere existence, social division of labor containing the seeds of oppression, antagonisms between groups of human beings and their eruption into violent conflict, and an incorrect understanding of the motive forces in nature and in society—things which have existed among human beings from the very earliest days—all this will be eliminated, surpassed. But as a leap forward, communism will not mean the total or one-sided negation of things from the past. Rather, it will mean that the products and experience of previous human history will be drawn from and recast to achieve a new synthesis through the cooperative association of human beings free of social antagonism and consciously applying a unified, comprehensive, scientific world outlook.

Changing Society, Changing "Human Nature"

In bringing this to a conclusion I want to speak again to the question of "human nature" and what historical materialism has to say about this.

As we have seen, it is one of the most cherished and widely used arguments of upholders of the bourgeois system that "human nature" cannot be changed; that the fundamental defect in communism and the fundamental reason for its "failure" is its attempt to change "human nature"; that human beings are by nature selfish, that they are by nature bound to seek their own individual interests above collective interests; and that it is only in giving free expression to the pursuit of individual interest by each against all that a higher good can somehow be served. Here another comment by Marx is very illuminating. He pointed out that this view merely reflects the production relations of bourgeois society itself and not some unchanging nature of human beings throughout history. He made the specific point that the bourgeois political economists assume that the production relations of capitalism are somehow eternal, or in any case that they are the final point of evolution of human production relations, and that any changes in society can only be made within the confines and on the basis of these production relations. But historical materialism reveals that not only these production relations but the ideas that correspond to them—including ideas about the "unchangeability of human nature"—are in fact historically limited, are the product of only a certain stage in the development of human history, and will be surpassed by the further advance of the class struggle and thereby the liberation of the productive forces of society, first and above all, the masses of laboring people.

Historical materialism makes clear that there is no such thing as innate, unchanging "human nature." What seems rational and natural is not the same in all ages and among all classes: it changes with a change in social conditions; and, in class society, it always reflects a definite class outlook (recall Marx's comment about how in the future communist society it will seem as absurd—or unnatural—for anyone to privately own the land as it does today for one person to own another; and recall also the point made earlier that the question of whether slavery appears "rational" and "natural" is bound to be answered differently by the slavemasters than by the slaves). Historical materialism and Marxism-Leninism-Maoism as a whole make clear that the proletarian revolution can and will bring about a profound change, an unprecedented change, in the relations among people and in the thinking of people, in their morality and motivations.

Historical Materialism and Making History

As discussed earlier, Engels explained why, until now, there have been certain common characteristics to human society and to the attitudes of people in society (what has been termed "human nature"): this is owing to the fact that up until the present time there has not been the basis to eliminate scarcity and the struggle for individual existence. But now, as Engels said, this basis has been established. Now, not only is it unnecessary for there to exist relations in which one part of society dominates and exploits another, but the persistence of such relations is an actual and direct hindrance to the further liberation of the productive forces and, above all, of the people. Now a social revolution is possible—and urgently demanded—to move humanity beyond all that and to a new stage of human history. (See Engels, "Socialism: Utopian and Scientific," *MESW*, v. 3, pp. 148-50.)

Today we stand at the threshold of a new era: bringing this new stage of human history into being is the historic task the communist revolution must and will fulfill. This is what historical materialism, and indeed all of Marxism-Leninism-Maoism, makes clear.

People need *materialism*! And this need is expressed acutely in today's world situation. It expresses itself very dramatically in relation to major world events and to the distorted view of them presented by the imperialists. People need dialectical materialism and its application to human society—historical materialism. They need to grasp the class relations, the class interests underlying things, for as Lenin put it:

"People always were and always will be the foolish victims of deceit and self-deceit in politics until they learn to discover the *interests* of some class or other behind all moral, religious, political and social phrases, declarations and promises. The supporters of reforms and improvements will always be fooled by the defenders of the old order until they realize that every old institution, however barbarous and rotten it may appear to be, is maintained by the forces of some ruling classes." (Lenin, "The Three Sources and Three Component Parts of Marxism," in *Marx, Engels, Marxism*, Peking, FLP, p. 73)

Beyond that, people must also understand what is the underlying foundation of these class relations and what is necessary to abolish class divisions and antagonisms. This is expressed in a pithy and powerful way in what is known as the "four all's"— which were put forward by Marx in a famous statement in which he said that the socialist revolution and the dictatorship of the proletariat represent the transition to "the *abolition of class distinctions generally*, to the abolition of all the relations of production on which they rest, to the abolition of all the social relations that correspond to these relations of production, to the revolutionizing of all the ideas that result from these social relations" (Marx, *MESW*, "The Class Struggles in France, 1848 to 1850," p. 282).

These "four all's" must be popularized, especially in these times, to give a clear, basic sense of what communism means and involves. They should be popularized in both senses: they should be made known broadly among the masses of people; and, while sometimes using these formulations exactly as Marx stated them in order to familiarize people with them, they should also be translated into more common terms. In this way, people will get the essence of what this is about and take it up as their own, so that through all the struggle of today they will be fired with the vision of what these "four all's" represent.*

People need the sweep that only the dialectical materialist outlook and methodology of Marxism-Leninism-Maoism can give them—an understanding of historical development and its underlying motive forces (contradictions). It is this outlook and methodology that can enable the masses of people to grasp the fact that, through all its complexity and its tortuous course of development, there is in human history the "coherence" of which Marx spoke. It is this outlook and methodology that can arm them with the ability to recognize the potential that now exists, precisely because of previous historical development, for a radical rupture with—a liberating leap beyond—all previous property relations and their corresponding institutions and ideas. It is this outlook and methodology that can inspire and embolden them to act to bring this into being—to consciously struggle to carry out and carry through the communist revolution worldwide.

It is this that gives substance and life to the slogans "Revolution Is the Hope of the Hopeless"; "Serve the People"; and "Fear Nothing, Be Down for the Whole Thing." It is this we must popularize. We must seize every opening to bring this forward in opposition to the foul and degrading outlook of the ruling powers and the old order they uphold. And even while today our focus, politically, is on the destruction of the old world, we must bring forward a vision and the seeds of the new world, including in the ideology we uphold and the way in which we give living expression to that ideology.

As Mao Tsetung said:

"A Communist should have largeness of mind and he should be staunch and active, looking upon the interests of the

---

* In connection with all this, and in particular on the relation between historical materialism and "the dirty little secret of capitalism," it is interesting to note a statement by Engels in *Anti-Dühring* that was cited by Stalin in "Economic Problems of Socialism." Engels pointed out that, in order to make a thorough critique of bourgeois economy, it was not enough to have an acquaintance with the capitalist form of production, exchange and distribution; it was also necessary to examine the forms which preceded capitalism or existed alongside it in the less developed countries. This was important in enabling people to put capitalism in perspective and in its true light, and therefore to see *beyond* it. (See Stalin, *Economic Problems of Socialism in the U.S.S.R.*, Peking, FLP, p. 73.)

revolution as his very life and subordinating his personal interests to those of the revolution; always and everywhere he should adhere to principle and wage a tireless struggle against all incorrect ideas and actions, so as to consolidate the collective life of the Party and strengthen the ties between the Party and the masses; he should be more concerned about the Party and the masses than about any private person, and more concerned about others than about himself." (Mao, "Combat Liberalism," *SW*, v. 2, p. 33)

And, as the Constitution of our Party sets forth, the basic orientation for communists and the first requirement for Party members is that they must:

"Keep constantly in mind, base themselves wholeheartedly on and dedicate their whole lives to the proletarian revolution and the historic mission of the international proletariat: the achievement of communism throughout the world." ("Constitution of the Revolutionary Communist Party, USA, Membership, Article 3, 1," in *New Programme and New Constitution of the Revolutionary Communist Party, USA*, p. 118)

Let the bourgeoisie, old and new, cling to the old order and declare that humanity can do no better. We know better. The proletarians, more than ever, have a world to win, a new world to bring into being, and in so doing they will emancipate not only themselves but all humanity.

Mao More Than Ever!

Long Live Marxism-Leninism-Maoism!

Phony Communism Is Dead, Long Live Real Communism!

ABOUT BOB AVAKIAN

"There's nothing about the present order of things in the world that is tolerable to me. It's completely intolerable. And I don't want to make my peace with it. I'm driven by an impatience with the world as it is, by an overwhelming sense that it has to be changed, and that the pace of change has to be accelerated. I feel an urgent burning desire to see everything radically changed, and I've come to understand that communist revolution holds the way to do this."

Bob Avakian is Chairman of the Revolutionary Communist Party, USA (RCP). A veteran of the revolutionary upsurges of the 1960s and 1970s, he worked closely with the Black Panther Party and was a major figure in the debates within the Students for a Democratic Society. He was instrumental in moving many activists towards Marxism-Leninism-Maoism and linking up with the working class.

By the mid-1970s, Avakian emerged as the foremost Maoist revolutionary in the United States. Today he heads the only party in the U.S. calling for and seriously working towards the overthrow of U.S. imperialism and its replacement by proletarian rule, socialism.

As revolutionary theoretician, Bob Avakian has given himself to solving the burning issues of making revolution. He has written numerous books and articles which have addressed such questions as: the relation of the Black people's struggle in the U.S. to proletarian revolution; the question of who in U.S. society really proletarian revolution; the question of who in U.S. society really represents a base for revolution and how political work can be conducted in a way that will prepare the ground for an organized revolutionary uprising; and, most recently, the challenge of how a revolutionary army could defeat a modern imperialist power. At the same time, Bob Avakian has confronted and offered penetrating insights into the historical problems and contradictions involved in carrying forward the proletarian revolution towards its goal of classless, communist society.

Certain individuals come forward at decisive hours to defend and uphold the banner of revolution. Bob Avakian is such a leader and thinker. In 1976, when the forces opposed to Mao Tsetung seized power in China, Avakian exposed that coup and made a thorough analysis of the causes and lessons of this counter-revolution. Today, as exploiters and reactionaries proclaim the "death of communism," Avakian has once again stepped forward to face the difficult questions of the day and to chart the path forward.

Bob Avakian takes revolution seriously. It should therefore come as no surprise that the authorities have hounded him with legal and extra-legal persecution. In 1980, under the threat of more than a lifetime in jail—as a result of trumped-up charges stemming from a demonstration against Deng Xiaoping in 1979—Bob Avakian was forced into exile in France.